Understanding Seed:
The Real Truth About the Harvest

by
Louis F. Kayatin

Vincom, Inc.
Tulsa, Oklahoma

Understanding Seed:
The Real Truth About the Harvest
ISBN 0-927936-61-5
Copyright ©1994 by
Louis F. Kayatin
Church on the North Coast
4125 Leavitt Road (Rt. 58)
Lorain, OH 44053-2399
(216) 960-1100

Published by
Vincom, Inc.
P. O. Box 702400
Tulsa, OK 74170
(918) 254-1276

Dedication

I would like to dedicate this work to my lovely wife, Tina, who is my closest friend and co-laborer in Christ. She is a constant encouragement to me.

Thank you for being my friend, wife and sister in the Lord.

Contents

Foreword

I am told that there are three kinds of people in this world — people who make things happen, people who watch things happen and people who do not know what is happening. Louis F. Kayatin belongs to the first group of people. He makes things happen.

In a day when most people simply point at problems of this life, Louis Kayatin is dedicated to offering solutions to seemingly hopeless situations.

Louis Kayatin has been called of God to bridge the gap between people of all ethnic backgrounds and to make a mark in their lives that cannot be erased.

God has uniquely anointed Louis Kayatin to explain and give insight on Old Testament passages and how they relate with the New Testament and day-to-day living.

His insights from God's World are extremely practical, yet exciting revelations that will impact your life for time to come.

Many have talked about seedtime and harvest, but very few have discussed putting the sickle to the harvest. This new and exciting book is sure to set your soul on fire.

Understanding Seed is a book that should be required reading for every Christian. Pastor Kayatin will give insight on the word *SICKLE* by using each letter to explain our responsibilities to help and assist in bringing in the harvest.

Once you read this book, you will come to the place of understanding how important it is to put the sickle to the harvest. I highly recommend it!

Creflo A. Dollar, Jr.
Senior Pastor
World Changers Ministries
College Park, Georgia

1

God Taught Adam
How To Prosper

**And God said, Behold, I have given you every herb
bearing seed, which is upon the face of all the earth,
and every tree, in the which is the fruit of a tree
yielding seed; to you it shall be for meat.**

Genesis 1:29

In the first chapter of Genesis, God spelled out His
principles of reproduction and prosperity.

He said to Adam, "This is My system, and this is
how the earth will produce fruit. Do you see this plant?
It has 'yielding' seed in it; it has the potential to
reproduce itself. It is not just a one-time plant or tree.
It will continue to grow and multiply. Eat some, and
save some to re-plant."

God showed Adam that when He planted that
seed, he could expect a harvest. Adam could expect to
reap what he had sown, and still have more than
enough to sustain himself. God created the earth with
the ability to not only replenish itself, but to multiply.
(Gen. 1:28.) God created the earth to increase and not
ever decrease.

One of the objections heard most often to the
message of increase is that it will not work all over
the world — and that is true. It will not work where

1

people worship rats and cows, trees and stones, and gods of the underworld and other demons. Not only will it not work in those places, but famine will come to that land.

We are hearing of a resurgence of prosperity in parts of India and Africa today. That is because people are turning away from idols and toward God. A national newspaper said in March, 1994, that a twelve-year drought in northern Africa is ending.

Madison Avenue does not teach us how to increase. God teaches His children how to prosper and increase. He gave Adam the ability to harvest his provision through understanding the seed. Like Adam, we must understand the seed and work God's principles in faith in order to gain our harvest.

What you lack in your life is a direct reflection of your understanding of seed. Are you experiencing lack of finances? Are you experiencing loneliness? Are you experiencing sickness? Are you experiencing a lack of joy? Your lack is in direct relationship to your understanding of planting seed in those areas.

Nearly every morning of my life, I plant health in my healthy body. I do not wait to be sick to pray. Instead, I pray for myself to remain healthy.

I look in the mirror and say things like, "Look! You are walking in health, and by Jesus' stripes you *were* healed. (1 Pet. 2:24.) I curse any type of virus in my blood system that might be trying to take over my body. I refuse to allow bacteria and germs to have dominance over my well-being. I thank You, Father, for Your provision of healing and divine health."

I am planting seeds of God's Word into my body. If sickness did come, I have a harvest of health with which to combat it. My walk with God is an active walk, a conscious walk. I sow seed into my relationships all of the time. In order to avoid marriage difficulties, you must sow seeds of a good marriage in order to reap the harvest.

If you are sick or hurting, pray for someone else. That way you are sowing seeds of healing, and what you sow, you will reap. Whatever "bread" you cast on the waters it will come back to you. (Eccles. 11:1.) Jesus also gave us the principles of planting and harvesting seed.

> For with what judgment ye judge, ye shall be judged: and with what measure ye mete, it shall be measured to you again.
>
> Matthew 7:2

> . . . With what measure ye mete, it shall be measured to you: and unto you that hear shall more be given.

> For he that hath, to him shall be given: and he that hath not, from him shall be taken even that which he hath.
>
> Mark 4:24,25

Seed Is Not Limited to Money

Seed is not limited to money. The Apostle Paul identified what our seed is in Galatians 3:16 AMP:

> Now the promises (covenants, agreements) were decreed and made to Abraham and his Seed (his Offspring, his Heir). He (God) does not say, And to seeds (descendants, heirs), as if referring to many persons; but, And to your Seed (your Descendant, your Heir), obviously referring to one individual, Who is [none other than] Christ, the Messiah. [Gen. 13:15; 17:8.]

If you see prosperity simply in terms of money, then you are not truly understanding the concept of "seed planting and harvesting."

It is not giving $5 and saying, "I'm planting this seed, and I am going to name what I need in return."

You cannot say, "I need a friend, so I am going to give $5."

You do not buy friendship, but you can "sow" for friendship by giving your own friendship to others.

The church must guard against erroneous teaching aimed at selfish gain.

Christ was the promised Seed. *Christ* means "the Anointed One." And Jesus Christ is also our Seed, because He is the Word of God made flesh. (John 1:1-3,14.)

If you do have lack in your life in any area, then you must find the right "Seed" to sow. You must find what the *Word of God* says about the area of lack, so that when you plant the Word, you will gain a harvest of that which you have planted.

This is not a theoretical message.

This is not a "let's-try-it-and-see" message.

This is not a message for you to take on faith in my word.

This book is based on a proven principle from the Word of God that has been used successfully in my own life and in the development of my church. Three years ago, we were giving $17,000 a year to missions. Then, when we got hold of a true understanding of sowing and reaping and that the Word of God is our seed, within a year, we were able to give $17,000 a month to world evangelism!

This year, we are up to about $22,000 a month. I can tell you from personal experience, and so can the people in my church, that this is not just another "prosperity message." Our church is in an economically depressed area, but I believe we are going to see prosperity come into our area and our city, as this message spills over into the community.

They understand that if they plant with finances, they sow into a ministry. However, I also make sure the people understand that sowing and reaping is not confined to money. Do not limit your understanding of the seed to any one area of your life.

Look at Deuteronomy 11:10-12 AMP:

> For the land which you go in to possess is not like the land of Egypt, from which you came out, where you sowed your seed and watered it with your foot laboriously, as a garden of vegetables;

> But the land, which you enter to possess, is a land of hills and valleys, and drinks water of the rain of the heavens;

> A land for which the Lord your God cares; the eyes of the Lord your God are always upon it, from the beginning of the year to the end of the year.

The life you are now living with Christ is not like the life you used to live without Him. It is a different life than the one you live with Jesus.

Our Seed Is Anointed

God was saying to the Israelites, "The land I am giving you is not like the land of Egypt where you used to sow your seed. You used to live by the sweat of your brow, making bricks with straw under the heavy hand of the taskmaster. You were sowing seed, but you were doing it *out of your own strength*. You were having to irrigate it with your foot.

"You had to make some kind of waterway to that seed to moisten its shell so that its potential could be fulfilled. That seed had to be cultivated so that it would erupt, break forth from the ground like a shoot, then bud and develop into the full fruit before the sun scorched it. Then, instead of getting a hundred pomegranates, you got one and were happy to get it."

Our "Seed" is already moistened, or anointed. It is anointed from Heaven. (Acts 10:38.)

God said the land He gave the Israelites was special to Him. He cared for it, and His eyes were on it from the beginning of the year to the end. In Kingdom sowing and reaping, you do not have to energize it with your ability. God says He will energize the Seed with His ability. It is called *anointing*. The Holy Spirit is able to go where we cannot in order to give us knowledge and to give us ability to do what we cannot do.

The Word of God is anointed with the power and dynamics of God, and when you sow it into your circumstances, He produces a harvest. Do not be embarrassed to take your harvest.

God's Word is powerful, and we should be proud to show off the results of our "Father's" Word. The Creator of the Universe teaches us to increase.

> Thus says the Lord, your Redeemer, the Holy One of Israel: I am the Lord your God Who teaches you to profit, Who leads you by the way that you should go.
>
> Isaiah 48:17 AMP

God teaches us how to increase and how to profit. The Bible does not say that He teaches us to fail, to decrease, to lose, or how to be sick and die prematurely. Verse 17 is a Kingdom principle. The very next verse says there is a condition, however, and that is: "Keeping His commandments."

If you pay attention to His commandments, He will bless you like a flowing river.

> **Oh, that you had hearkened to My commandments! Then your peace and prosperity would have been like a flowing river; and your righteousness [the holiness and purity of the nation] like the abundant waves of the sea.**
>
> **Isaiah 48:18 AMP**

Keeping God's commandments means being faithful with your seed planting. God will trust you with little friendships, and whether or not He trusts you with friendships later that have great implications for you depends on how faithful you are with the little ones. The same is true in any area, including finances.

If you plant seeds of discord, you will reap discord.

If you do not want to be misunderstood, do not misunderstand other people.

If you want to be esteemed and valued, then esteem and value other people. Operate in the laws of the Word of God.

When God told Noah to build the ark, He made sure that Noah had two of each kind in order for the seed of each kind to be preserved along with the "soil" in which that seed could reproduce.

2
Four Steps From Seed to Harvest

> **And his disciples asked him, saying, What might this parable be?**
>
> **Now the parable is this** (Jesus answered): **The seed is the word of God.**
>
> **Luke 8:9,11**

As I began to study sowing seed and reaping, I found there were almost three hundred scriptures in the Bible that deal with *seed*. As I went through these verses, I meditated on each one to extract God's thinking about sowing seed for a bountiful harvest. I saw that some things I had believed — and even said before — were not quite right, because I had not attained a clear understanding.

There are four applications that must be done in order to reap a harvest. There are four main steps that a farmer goes through from seed to harvest. Spiritual sowing and reaping follow the same procedures. These are:

1. Preparing the soil to receive the seed
2. Planting the seed
3. Watering and protecting the seed
4. Waiting patiently for the right time to harvest

In the first chapter, we saw what the Seed that should be sown in all areas is: Jesus Christ, the Word

9

made flesh. So planting the promises or the verses in the Bible that apply to every area in our lives is *planting the Living Word*.

First Peter 1:23-25 says:

> **Being born again, not of corruptible seed, but of incorruptible, by the word of God, which liveth and abideth for ever.**

> **For all flesh is as grass, and all the glory of man as the flower of grass. The grass withereth and the flower thereof falleth away:**

> **But the word of the Lord endureth for ever. And this is the word which by the gospel is preached unto you.**

That is important for you to know. You must understand that the Word of God will not perish. It is not something that will falter in the middle of its "growth cycle." It is not something that pesticide can destroy or some crisis or calamity can wipe out, such as the great flood that destroyed the harvests of much of the Midwest in 1993.

This Seed is imperishable. You cannot destroy it. That is important to know so that you can have confidence in the planting process and not be wondering whether or not your seed is going to make it. Of course, it will make it, because God said the Word will not return void. (Isa. 55:11.)

Peter was saying, "Listen, things will come, and things will go, but the Word of God goes on forever. It will never pass away."

The Word of God is the best seed that exists. For a clear understanding of preparing your seed, look at a parable Jesus told, as recorded in the gospel of Luke.

A sower went out to sow his seed: and as he sowed, some fell by the way side; and it was trodden down, and the fowls of the air devoured it.

And some fell upon a rock; and as soon as it was sprung up, it withered away, because it lacked moisture.

And some fell among thorns; and the thorns sprang up with it, and choked it.

And other fell on good ground, and sprang up, and bare fruit an hundredfold. And when he had said these things, he cried, He that hath ears to hear, let him hear.

Luke 8:5-8

The disciples did not understand this parable any more than did the Pharisees and the multitudes who were listening to Jesus. He explained to them that those by the wayside are those who hear but allow the devil to steal the "seed" from the soil of their hearts. (Luke 8:12.)

The rocky ground on which some seed fell, Jesus said, are those hearts who believe for a little while, but fall away in the time of temptation. And the "thorns" among which some seed falls are those who allow what they have heard to be choked out by the cares and the pleasures of this life, so that no fruit comes forth. (Luke 8:13,14.)

To "prepare the soil," you must prepare your heart to take in the Word of God and allow it to take root in you, and to become part of you.

Preparing the Soil

Pastors say that churches and ministries are "good soil," and that can be true; however, when I used to say that, I did not have full revelation of God's plan and principle. You can sow into a church or ministry.

You can sow service, talents, gifts, and finances. But that is not the full revelation of either the seed or the soil.

According to the parable in Luke 8, the soil is the heart. The seed, the Word of God, when planted in the heart and watched over and protected, then watered by the Holy Spirit, will bring forth a harvest of whatever has been planted. When you "sow" services or finances into a church or ministry, it will not bring you a harvest *unless* you have first sowed the true Seed into your heart.

Your heart is the soil from which comes the harvest of a faith walk with God, your relationship with Jesus, and your ability to hear the direction of the Holy Spirit.

The Lord showed me an aspect of preparing the soil that is not often considered: Good soil is soil that is *decomposing*. In the natural, putting compost in your garden makes the soil a richer mix. For a victorious faith walk to result from seed planted in our hearts, the "old man" (Col. 3:9) — whom the Apostle Paul talked about in each of us — must die.

This is why we are told to "walk by faith and not by sight." (2 Cor. 5:7.) *Sight* represents the old man, and *faith* represents the decomposing of the old man that actually provides nutrients for growth in the new man. If you have ever cultivated a garden or been around someone who did, then you know that the best thing to make that garden grow is a load of manure. Perhaps you feel that you have had a load of manure (trials or tribulations) dumped on you in the last few months or years.

Perhaps you have said, "God, what did I do to derserve this?"

God says, "You deserve it. You are the one who asked Me for accelerated growth!"

Luke 8:15 says that good soil is "an honest and good heart" which hears the Word and brings forth fruit with *patience*. Some other translations say *perseverance*. It takes patience or perseverance to withstand the onslaught of manure, which does not feel good or smell good. In fact, it is repulsive.

Other people wonder what in the world is going on. They walk by you and try to avoid you. It seems as if your life is falling apart.

But God said, "What the devil meant for evil, I will turn for good."

So when the devil is laughing at the "manure" being poured on you, you ought to rejoice. James also wrote that we should rejoice when trials and tribulations come. (James 1:2-4.)

Jesus said, "In this world, you will have manure deliveries, but be of good cheer, for I have overcome them all." (John 16:33, my translation!)

Since understanding this, I am not too concerned about tribulation. Manure is not major concern for me any longer. I understand that it works to my good, because God is the Husbandman, the Farmer, and He knows what He is doing.

Also, if you look at the natural growth of a garden, you know that it takes no work to grow a crop of thorns and thistles. The processes of this world will "seed" thorns and thistles in our hearts without any efforts on our part. However, it takes a conscious effort and diligent work to prepare the soil in order for good seed to grow.

When I die to self, the decomposition of my life actually is enriching the soil. When I put the Word into my life, I am no longer carrying out the desires of the flesh. It is important to live by the Word, not by religious traditions or the world's knowledge.

This world is under a curse and will produce death automatically. (Gen. 3:17.) The only way to reverse the curse is to sow that which is above the curse. If you sow the Word into that which was cursed, the curse has to give way to life. *Death gives way to life.* The only way you can defeat the natural harvest of death is to sow life.

Jesus said His words are spirit and life. (John 6:63.) And James wrote that the "power of life and death" are in the tongue. (James 3:5,6; Prov. 18:21.)

Identifying the types of soil we are is descriptive of the interference in our Christian lives from our past lives. In addition to allowing the decomposing of the old man to help the seed (the Word) grow in us, we must remove the "rocks."

We cannot walk the faith walk with rocks on the road. Did you ever try to walk where there is gravel of various sizes. It is very difficult to get a sound footing, so in this sense, you must remove those obstacles that choke the seed in your heart.

"Thorns" then must be pulled up in order to have good soil. Thorns and thistles are nothing more than fears and doubts.

Planting the Seed

Leviticus 19:19 says not to mix your seed when you plant. In other words, do not plant wheat and barley together or soybeans and corn. Plant one crop. Keep your harvest pure. For example, planting a seed that you hope will result in a bountiful harvest, but mixing it with the seed of fear (thorns), may result in little or no returns. "Thorns" of fear will choke out faith.

Another key is to "sow bountifully." (2 Cor. 9:6.) Paul wrote that the person who sows sparingly will reap sparingly. The Church today sows sparingly, because it costs too much to sow bountifully. Sowing few seeds means a stunted harvest.

Also, many Christians are not sowing the Word of God in various areas of their lives because it takes effort, diligence, and patience. Any good farmer knows that it is all right if you have to work sixteen or eighteen hours a day during planting time, because the harvest is going to be worth it.

A good farmer knows that little things he might ordinarily enjoy will have to be set aside during certain seasons. He might like to see Monday night football, but if he does not get his seed in the ground, fertilize that field, keep out the weeds, and water the plants, he will never see the harvest.

In Ecclesiastes 3, there is a list of things that the writer tells us have various set times. He said there is a time to plant and a time to reap. When you are sowing, do not play or feast. After you harvest, then you can feast.

The problem with many Christians today is that they just want the harvest. They do not want to sweat and plant and smell manure. God is calling us to do some work. He is calling us to sow seriously, to make an effort.

Find where the area of lack is in your life, then find the "seed" to plant there from the Word of God. After that, you must plan times when you can consistently sow that Word — not on the side of the road, not on rocky places, not with thorns, but in good soil.

That means *you must die* to the things of the old nature, the pre-Jesus life, that you have not been able to die to before. You must endure with perseverance the loads of manure that are dumped on your soil, because in due season, you will reap if you do not faint. (Gal. 6:9.)

Christians today are not that serious about the Word. But we had better get serious, because there is a generation out there that is going to be looking for help.

They will be saying, "Do any of these churches have anything real? Are there churches that can sustain us? We thought you people believed in the Bible."

Another thing that will assist your crop is to plant with joy. God loves a cheerful giver. (2 Cor. 9:7.) That does not mean getting emotional in church when offering time comes. Paul was talking about the cheerfulness that comes even though what you are doing is hard work, because you know what the end result will be.

You need to be excited about sowing seed, excited about what God is going to do: "Come and see the seed I have found in the Word of God to plant! Come and look at what I expect in my harvest!"

You must have a *strategy and a plan*. So many times, we abort our harvests. Or we let it rot in the fields because we have no barns in which to store it. We have not thought about the future. We just go through life haphazardly hoping things will work out, and we will get to Heaven some day.

Instead of understanding that "manure" is necessary for growth, we try to get out from under it. We try to avoid all the crises and disasters in life.

In 2 Corinthians 9:8, Paul wrote that God is able to make all grace abound to us so that we will have, not just a sufficiency, but an abundance for every good work. I am saddened by Christians not having an abundance.

There ought to be more than enough encouragement to young people who grow up in a Christian home.

There ought to be more than enough money to do ministry or fund missions or give faithful workers in the Lord's vineyard a raise or even a little something extra.

There ought to be more than enough volunteers to carry out the work of the churches, ministries, and missions.

It is wrong to say that it is God's will that we are not living in abundance! God's Word and His will are the same, and He has made it crystal clear that He wants us to have an abundance for every good deed.

Jesus gave to the poor, but He did not give them money that would be here today and gone tomorrow. He gave them the Word of God. The government wants to help the poor, but instead of teaching them how to read or how to work, they give them money. And the next month, they have to give the same people more money. It is a vicious cycle of defeat.

Water and Protect the Seed

The watering process is something a child of God does not have to do. The Word of God is like rain when it is spoken out into the atmosphere. When the Word of God is spoken into the soil, which is faith in our hearts, it *will* produce. Rain makes the ground produce. God gives the harvest, the increase. Our part is to prepare the soil, plant the seed, and then harvest the fruits for God.

Paul wrote in 1 Corinthians 3:6-8:

> **I have planted, Apollos watered; but God gave the increase.**

> **So then neither is he that planteth any thing, neither he that watereth; but God that giveth the increase.**

> **Now he that planteth and he that watereth are one: and every man shall receive his own reward according to his own labour.**

You may say, "You mean God does not need my watering?"

No, He does not. Paul was telling us that God is going to cause the growth because He has a built-in irrigation system in the seed. The *seed* is already watered.

Remember in Galatians 3:16, Paul wrote that Christ is the Seed, and John wrote that Christ is the Word made flesh. So the *seed* that we are to plant is the *anointed* Word of God.

Joel wrote that in the last days, God would send both the early and the latter rain upon the Seed. (Joel 2:23.) Those who are planting seed are going to see an endtime harvest which the world has never seen — an accelerated harvest, an increased harvest — because the former and the latter rain will be poured out together on the Word.

If Christians really understood this, they would be getting rocks out of their lives, thorns of fear pulled up, and asking God to help accelerate the decomposing process of their old natures. We need to get off the edges of the road and get into the middle of what God is doing. His Spirit is being poured out upon all flesh for one purpose: to increase the realized revelation of the Word of God in the last days.

The Kingdom of God is not coming together in big crowds for seminars and marking up your Bible. Jesus said the Kingdom is like a man who takes seed and casts it on the soil. Then he goes to bed at night, gets up by day, and how the seed sprouts up and grows, he does not know. (Mark 4:27.)

When Jesus said for us not to be anxious for anything, He was saying to just cast your seed on the soil and "go to bed," so to speak. Do not worry about the harvest. Do not keep pulling up your seed to see if it has sprouted.

How do you pull up the seed? You do that when you adopt other words besides those you planted. You pull it up by the root to see if it is growing when you question the seed you planted. God told Joshua that if he would meditate on the law (the Word of God) day and night, he would have success wherever he went. (Josh. 1:8.)

God is the One Who gives the increase. I give my decomposing, carnal life for the spiritual walk. My faith is mixed with patience which perseveres, is consistent, and leaves the seed in the ground. I do not allow myself to act or feel defeated. Then, suddenly, the soil causes that seed to sprout. The soil, if it is good ground and prepared well, produces crops by itself. God gives the increase.

I am so glad I do not have to recite formulas or do some religious exercise to expedite its growth. First, comes the blade, then the ear, then the full ear of corn, Jesus said. (Mark 4:28.)

In John 4:14, Jesus told the woman at the well in Samaria that anyone who drank of the water He gave would never thirst. The "water" that was given to us when we became born again is the "well of water springing up into everlasting life," Jesus said. (John 4:14.)

The Seed planted in you at the new birth contains the eternal water of God. It will produce a "well of salvation." (Isa. 12:3.)

God was saying, "I have given you a Word (Jesus) that has an encasement of water that will take care of its growth. However, you do have one part in the watering process: You must *keep your soil wet*. The well is already in you, but you can let it run dry. The well is still there (you are still saved), but the life you live on earth can become like desert land.

Any Dryness Is Not in the Seed

As the seed grows, if there is any dryness to be concerned with, it is not in the *seed* (the Word), which has the built-in moisture of the anointing from God, it is in the *soil*. The Word of God will never get dry.

Jesus said that the person who believes in Him will have rivers of water flowing out of his "belly" (his heart, or spirit). So how do you keep the soil wet?

• You keep the soil wet by staying in close fellowship with the Lord, and you do that by allowing the Holy Spirit to decompose all of the old ways, habits, attitudes, and behaviors in you.

• You keep the soil wet by not sinning, by not continuing in the old ways.

• You keep the soil wet by staying in the Word and "meditating on it day and night," as the Lord told Joshua. (Josh. 1:8.)

Look at 1 Kings 8:35, where God said the heavens were shut up and there was no rain *because the people had sinned against Him.* When you sin, it will not rain, and seed will not grow.

There is a stronger emphasis being placed on sanctification in the Christian world today. Christians are realizing that the state of this country is becoming desert, dry and barren, because more and more sin has been tolerated. The only remedy is to return to God so that America can again have rain. God wants to pour out the former and the latter rain on His people.

You must hold onto the Word and not lose your confidence. When you are preparing the soil, you must "plow" it with the Word and allow the "manure" to enrich it. But you also must protect the seed once it is planted in the fertilized soil. The devil will try to dive right down in the bed of your garden and rip the seed right out of the ground.

In the parable in Luke, Jesus said that people in whom the seed has not taken firm root will fall away when persecution or affliction comes. Instead of allowing that to decompose the old things in them that cause wrong reactions to people and circumstances, they fall away from the way of God.

Just like that, which Jesus used as an analogy of salvation, the same thing can happen with seeds of the Word planted in faith in other areas of your life. If you plant a seed of finances, services, or love and friendship, you have to protect it from the thorns of fear and doubt and from the devil's dive-bomb attacks, which the Bible calls "fiery darts." (Eph. 6:16.)

I saw a television program once on a certain kind of bird that builds its nest on the ground. The father bird builds the nest out of vegetation that decomposes. The eggs are pushed down into this mass of compost, and he keeps the temperature stable by taking some material out or adding some. The more it decomposes, the warmer the soil gets.

Most attackers cannot steal the eggs, because they cannot see them. So "hide" your seed from the eyes of people who are full of doubts and fears and whose words might "destroy" your seed. However, there is one adversary who knows those seeds have been planted.

In the nature program, there was a bird that came along with a great, long beak. It thrust its beak through the nest and ate the eggs or the little birds after they hatched. You defend your eggs from the enemy with the great, long beak through prayer and fasting.

He also might lure you off the nest with a desire for possessions, entertainments, and ideas of the world's systems. Jesus called those "the deceitfulness of riches" and "the desires of other things." (Mark 4:19.) Those will choke out the Word, or stunt the growth of the seed.

You protect the seed by standing with patience and perseverance, and refusing to be moved or lured away from your seed.

You protect your seed by driving away those birds of prey that would steal it. In Genesis 15:11, Abraham and God were making a blood covenant, the planting of the *seed* for the eventual redemption of mankind and

the restoration of all things. Birds of prey came down
on the carcasses of the sacrifices spread out as part of
the covenant-cutting process, and the Bible says that
Abram drove them away. Likewise, we must drive Satan
away from our crops.

Expectancy Is the Breeding Ground of Miracles

The fourth step in the process of moving from
seed-planting to harvest is to *wait with patience* after you
have done all that you can do. Paul wrote that we need
the whole armor of God in order to withstand in the
evil day. And, he said, when we have done all that we
can, we must simply just *stand*.

> **Stand therefore, having your loins girt about with
> truth, and having on the breastplate of righteousness;**
>
> **And your feet shod with the preparation of the
> gospel of peace;**
>
> **Above all, taking the shield of faith, wherewith
> ye shall be able to quench all the fiery darts of the
> wicked.**
>
> **And take the helmet of salvation, and the sword
> of the Spirit, which is the word of God:**
>
> **Praying always with all prayer and supplication
> in the Spirit, and watching thereunto with all
> perseverance and supplication for all saints.**
>
> **Ephesians 6:14-18**

From those verses, we can see that you are not
standing unless you have on the *whole* armor of God.
You need more than a scarecrow in this kind of garden!
The thing you need above all, Paul wrote, is the shield
of faith. The Living Word of God, Jesus, is all things
to His children. In Him is everything needed for
salvation, health, and prosperity in all areas of our lives.

The written Word of God tells us what all of these things are which we have *in* and *from* Jesus.

Through faith in Him and what He did to defeat the works of Satan (1 John 3:8), we can find seeds in the written Word to plant, and the *same words* make a shield to defend the gardens of our hearts, as well as outward aspects of our daily lives.

However, there is a simpler way to have good soil that remains moist and is protected from the enemy. That is to have a heart that is enriched. The enriched soil of a Christian's heart is *love*. When you walk the love walk, it takes care of defense, offense, and maintenance problems. (1 Cor. 13.)

If you do not walk in love, it is very difficult not to sin. When you sin, it stops the waters from flowing out of you. But Paul wrote that *love never fails*.

If you even gossip about someone else, much less make malicious or sarcastic remarks, your soil has lost some of its moisture.

God wants His people to be raised up by denying the flesh and making the soil of their hearts rich, so that His seed planted will bring in a great harvest of fruit. Tears of repentance and intercession cause the rivers of water to flow. The Church should be planting those kinds of seed for the harvest of souls intended by God in the endtimes.

As a Church, we have done all the external things (activities, programs, conferences, and seminars), but our barns are empty. A generation of people are coming expecting to find food and to get their needs met, and many churches and Christians will have nothing to give them because they have let their soil become dry ground.

Part of standing is *rejoicing*. Joy in the Lord should be a part of each step of this process. Plant with joy and expectancy. Plant, knowing that God delights in the prosperity of His servant. (Ps. 35:27.) He delights in that because He knows that His servant is going to give Him all of the glory and honor.

The concept of *confession* that was taught extensively a few years ago was misunderstood. The true purpose of confessing something is not a formula to "claim" something, as if you have to take it away from God. Confessing is believing and rejoicing that God keeps His Word.

The first step, of course, is to find the seed in His Word that holds the harvest of what you need. Make sure the seed you need to plant is a legitimate seed in agreement with the will of God for you. Then plant and rejoice in advance over the harvest.

God gives us the moist seed to sow, but we must plant, protect, and wait with patience for the increase which He sends. Once we have the increase, we must know when to put in the sickle for the harvest. There is a right time to harvest, as well as a right time to sow seed.

The next chapter provides a strategy to enable you to harvest that which you have planted.

3

The Importance of the Sickle

**But when the fruit is brought forth, immediately
he putteth in the sickle, because the harvest is come.**
Mark 4:29

God said in Deuteronomy 11 that He had not given
the Israelites a land like the former land, the land of
Egypt, that had to be irrigated and worked over with
hard labor. Egypt is used in the Bible as a symbol or
picture of carnal living. Before you were saved, you
were in bondage in "Egypt," the world of the flesh.

What God told Israel concerning the promised
land was a spiritual picture of the difference between
the life of the flesh and the life of the Spirit. Our
promised land is the Kingdom of God, and if you are
living in that Kingdom without grumbling and com-
plaining and always wishing you were back in the
fleshpots of carnality, you can have an abundance of
everything.

The faith walk is a land watered from Heaven. If
we truly walked in love and faith, we should not have
to try to make ends meet. All we would do is sow the
seed, protect the seed, make sure our soil stays watered,
and wait for the harvest.

Remember that Jesus said the soil produces by
itself, and when the crop is ready, the farmer

immediately puts in the sickle. (Mark 4:29.) A *sickle* is a sharp blade with a long handle which was used from ancient times until even into the twentieth century to harvest grain. In America, sometimes it was called a "scythe." Today, we have huge machinery called combines.

A lot of Christians sow, and a lot of them get a harvest. But some do not always get the harvest into the barn. We need to understand how to get the harvest out of the field and into the barn. According to scripture, the *sickle* is the key. Without something to harvest with, your crops will rot in the fields.

As I was studying in order to understand God's seed, I felt He gave me the answers in an acrostic on the word *sickle*. (An acrostic is a word made up from the first letters of another word, phrase, or sentence.) Psalm 119 is a Biblical example. The first letter of each verse in Hebrew spells out the Hebrew alphabet from *aleph* to *tau* when you put them all together.

The Hebrews loved figures of speech, word games, and so forth; in other words, painting pictures with words. The Old Testament is very poetic.

The acrostic for sickle is this:

S — strategy
I — insight
C — cultivate
K — kinetics
L — love
E — endurance

The *sickle* is the key to the entire concept of the harvest.

God's will for your prosperity is found in 3 John 2.

Beloved, I wish above all things that thou mayest prosper and be in health, even as thy soul prospereth.

The *kind of seed* you sow determines the *kind of harvest* you reap. The verse the Lord gave me for the concept of naming your harvest was Jesus' comment about putting in the sickle. (Mark 4:29.)

Where people took that teaching into error is when they, in essence, claimed "pumpkins" out of "apple seed," or love out of sowing money. Also, error came in claiming something for which there is no seed, no promise or Word, to be found in the Bible.

When a farmer plants corn, he *names* his harvest: so many bushels of corn. He does not claim so many bushels of wheat from seed corn, or potatoes from tomato plants.

Prosperity in the Word of God means having abundance in every area of our lives. It does not mean that every Christian will be a millionaire or live in a million-dollar house. Prosperity in some places might mean a bicycle or a camel. The Bible also does not say that everyone will reap a hundred-fold. There are harvests of less returns.

The soil in which the seed is planted makes a difference.

The protection given the seed makes a difference.

The purity of the seed, whether it is mixed with weeds and thorns, makes a difference.

To go back to Jesus' words in Mark 4, He said that when the harvest is ready, the husbandman *immediately* puts in the sickle — which means that when he sowed the seed *he already had a plan*.

The Greek word translated *immediately* means "to thrust in exactly."

As soon as the harvest matured, then the farmer was ready to pull it in to put in his barns. And, obviously, he could not wait until he saw the harvest to get ready.

Prepare for the Harvest

Jesus was talking about a good, industrious farmer who knew his business and was diligent in preparing for all of the steps in the process of sowing and reaping. Here is what he did:

1. He *chose* the kind of seed for the result he wanted.

If you want a return in money, you plant money. And tithing is not sowing seed; it is giving God the only share He requires so that He may always have "meat" in His house. That means provisions for ministry. You cannot legitimately sow seed until you have given God His portion. Seed goes beyond tithe and offerings.

2. He prepared the soil and protected the growing plants, as we saw in the last chapter.

3. He prepared barns to hold the harvest.

4. He had tools or equipment in order to get in the harvest.

5. He not only had a sickle, but he had it on hand, sharpened and ready to use.

Your harvest may rot in the fields or dry up and blow away if you have to go hunt the sickle; and, because it is rusty from lying out in the field, you have to take time to sharpen it. Or, perhaps the handle is broken, and you have to make a new one and fit the blade on it.

This lack of preparation is what King Solomon called *slothfulness* in Proverbs.

> **I went by the field of the slothful, and by the vineyard of the man void of understanding;**
>
> **And, lo, it was all grown over with thorns, and nettles had covered the face thereof, and the stone wall thereof was broken down.**
>
> **So shall thy poverty come as one that travelleth; and thy want as an armed man.**
>
> **Proverbs 24:30,31,34**

Many Christians sow seed, then are slothful about keeping the soil watered, the weeds pulled up, and the birds scared off. Notice also that the man without understanding gets the same result as one who is slothful. That is why I feel this teaching on understanding seed is so important!

Many have never gotten harvests from their seeds and are falling away saying, "Well, this stuff doesn't work."

And the problem is that they simply did not understand that the *seed* they needed to sow was the Word that accompanied the money, services, or goods which they gave. They focused on *what* they sowed, not on the real Seed, and then were disappointed. Confessing the Word *is* the seed. But faith must be accompanied by works to be effective. So the real "invisible" Seed must surround a visible gift.

Sow the Word of God and back up your faith by giving into other people's ministries or lives, and your harvest will come in due season if you do not faint. (Gal. 6:9.)

Make a Plan, Have a Strategy

The Lord showed me that the first letter in sickle stands for *strategy*.

You must have a strategy before you even begin to sow or plant. Having a plan means not just scattering seed, not just throwing it anywhere, any place, any time. The first part of any successful strategy in the Kingdom of God is to have your main motive being *to honor God through your obedience.*

Tithing is obeying God in order for His ministry to proceed and His Kingdom to be extended. The reward or return that He promised is for the windows of Heaven to be opened, and blessings to be poured out that we would not have room enough to contain, that the devourer would be rebuked for our sakes; and that His people would be a "delightsome" land that other people would call blessed. (Mal. 3:10-12.)

None of that is sowing seed for a harvest. It is obedience, being a faithful servant, and doing what we ought to do as loving children of a loving Father.

King Solomon wrote something that helps us see where sowing begins:

> **Honour the Lord with thy substance, and with the firstfruits of all thine increase:**
>
> **So shall thy barns be filled with plenty, and thy presses shall burst out with new wine.**
>
> **Proverbs 3:9,10**

This is where harvest also begins: Honoring the Lord with *our* substance. Paying the tithe is honoring Him by obedience in giving Him what He has said already is His. Of course, not paying tithes becomes disobedience and dishonoring God, to say nothing of causing His work to suffer.

A little less than twenty percent of all Christians pay tithes. If they really believed the Word of God, they would know they were going to be held accountable for robbing God. (Mal. 3:8,9.)

If the Church does not get hold of this principle, people in the world are going to stay on drugs, stay in poverty, stay exploited by greed, and continue to go to Hell.

When you enable others to minister to people, you honor the Lord. When you give to the poor, you sow seed.

God wants our barns to be filled with plenty. He wants the harvest, the increase which He has brought, stored in our barns in order for us to plant more crops, have enough for ourselves, and share with those who are not as fortunate.

My strategy is not to work for a living, but *to work for giving*. My "living" will be taken care of because I honor the Lord with my giving. The Kingdom of God is sowing seed, Jesus said, so I want to have enough in my barns in addition to the tithe and my own food to give ("sow") when the Holy Spirit says, "Do this," or "Give that."

I look for opportunities to serve.

I look for opportunities to give money.

I look for ways to help bear others' burdens.

I look for ways to strengthen those who are weak.

I look for ways to implement the Word by sowing it into other people's lives.

That is my agenda in life. That is why I live and move. That is my strategy in "farming" the fields of this world.

My harvest gets bigger every day, because every time I harvest something, I sow more seed. Like many Christians, there was a time when I ate my seed. If I sowed something and got a couple of hundred dollars back, I put it on bills, or whatever. Of course, I tithed out of it, but I "ate up" the rest.

Then one day, the Lord said to me, "Why are you eating all of your seed?"

If you have enough harvest to make ten loaves of bread, and you give the Lord one, but eat nine, your next harvest is nonexistent, or it gets smaller. You should give the Lord His, then sow four loaves, and eat only five.

Part of getting a strategy is realizing why you are sowing, understanding what the purpose is for the harvest.

When people say, "I am naming my seed," they should be saying, "I am getting my sickle ready because I have planted this and I will reap more of this."

Insight From the Holy Spirit

Insight is wisdom gained from seeking the Holy Spirit on what you should do with the harvest. Not long ago, someone gave me $1,000. That represented a harvest on some money I had sown. At this point, I had gained insight into how God worked.

So I immediately put in my sickle and said, "Holy Spirit, how much do I sow for the next harvest?"

He said, "Give half."

I said, "Half? Well, okay, I will give half. Five hundred dollars is better than no hundred in my hand, is it not?"

Insight goes farther than that however. My next question was, "Who gets the half? Who am I supposed to give this to? Who am I supposed to bless?" This is where the sharpened sickle comes in.

Every day that goes by, we need insight into the plan of God for our seed, because the devil is going to try to get us to eat the seed. And, if we eat the seed, everything is over. There is no more potential for greater harvest, and each day that goes by, the devil has another opportunity to steal the seed.

Having *insight* means getting a dream or a vision from God concerning your destiny, the purpose He has for you in this life. We will talk more of this in the next chapter.

Most Christians live out their lives without a strategy, without insight, without a dream or a vision, and without an understanding of sowing and reaping.

Every ministry, as well as every Christian, ought to have a sharpened sickle ready at hand to harvest the increase from what they have sown.

You need to seek God for answers to these questions:

How can I cultivate my soil?

How can I till the soil around my crop?

How can I sharpen my sickle?

How can I improve my ability to transfer the harvest into the barn?

How can I fulfill my dream?

You sow seeds to fulfill your dream with the third word in our acronym: *cultivate*. This means first tilling, digging, hoeing, transplanting, thinning out, raking, or weeding *someone else's garden*.

The Kingdom of God works in such a way that, when you cultivate someone else's seed, your seed will be cultivated.

You may say, "I'm not doing that for someone else!"

Then stay poor, stay without friends, stay with a ministry of your own that never gets off the ground.

Insight is understanding how this works and finding the person the Holy Spirit wants you to help. Find out how you can make their dream or vision happen.

This generation will be the first in the history of this nation not to have things as good or better than the last generation. That is because we have forgotten how to sow. We have forgotten how to help others and have started relying on the government to do it. When the government tries to help everyone, they also *take* from everyone, and your sowing no longer is voluntary.

In fact, it no longer is *sowing*. It no longer is loving and helping your neighbor. It is paying taxes and more taxes. That is the "harvest" of self-centeredness and selfishness. In the Sixties, the winds of rebellion were sown in society, and today, we are reaping the whirlwind of that. (Hos. 8:7.)

Instead of working together in unity, most denominations and churches are waging war on one another, trying to prove one is better than the other. Christians are writing books that are guided missiles at certain ministries. If they only knew what they were sowing. The harvest will boomerang on them in a greater degree than they have sown.

The sad part is that our children will reap the harvest. We sow, and they reap.

The Harvest of Joseph

In the Bible, one of the great stories about sowing and reaping is that of Joseph, great-grandson of Abraham and beloved eleventh son of Jacob, who first was named Israel.

Joseph's brothers were jealous of him and sold him into slavery. He ended up in an Egyptian prison after he stood up for godly moral principles. After several years in jail, God's purposes in allowing this "load of manure" to fall into Joseph's life began to be clearly seen.

What the devil meant for evil had been turned by God for good for Joseph, his entire tribal family, and the Kingdom of God. God was able to turn it, because Joseph honored Him through his obedience and made choices according to God's will, including living a life of love under extremely harsh circumstances.

In Genesis 40, we read of Pharaoh's cupbearer, or butler, and chief baker who had been tossed into prison because they had offended him. While there, they had dreams that distressed them. Joseph had been put in charge of the prison, like a top trustee would be today. He came into the cell, or place, where these two men were one morning and found them looking sad.

It seems to us that anyone would be sad who was confined in prison now, much less the kind of prisons they had then. But there must have been something more than usual about the expressions of these two for Joseph to say, "Wherefore look ye so sadly to-day?" (v. 7.)

Joseph had every reason to be sad on his own account. His own brothers had rejected him to the point of selling him into slavery. He had been unjustly accused by his first owner's wife. (Gen. 39:7-20.) He had no reason for hope in the future. As far as he knew, he was in prison until he died.

Yet he began to sow into the welfare of this baker and cupbearer. He took an interest not only in their conditions but in the states of their minds. When he found their dejected feelings were because of a dream each of them had the night before, he told them to cheer up, because he would interpret those dreams.

A lot of us are in the same place as those who want our help. Instead of being like Joseph, we worry about ourselves and think we cannot help them because of our own situations.

We say, "Hey, I'm trying to get food on my table and pay my bills. I can't help you. Life is tough all over!"

Joseph's interpretation may not have been very cheering to the baker, whose dream of three baskets of good things being eaten by birds meant he was to be beheaded in three days. Or perhaps he was grateful at having three days to prepare for death. The Bible does not tell us.

Nevertheless, Joseph sowed and later received a harvest. Whether the other person's dream was fulfilled or not, Joseph had sowed into their lives.

Many denominations and independent churches will not give to others if they are not "one of us." The cupbearer was not one of Joseph's. He was an Egyptian, while Joseph was a Hebrew. Egyptians did not like Hebrews. They would not even associate with them. They would not even eat at the same table with them. (Gen. 43:32.)

Events turned out as Joseph had prophesied. The baker was beheaded in three days, but the chief butler was restored to favor. Then he did what so many of us do. When the trials are over, and we are restored, we forget about the people who helped us during the trials. A lot of times, we forget about thanking God for His help in those times. Two more years went by with Joseph stuck in prison before his harvest was ready.

Then God gave Pharaoh some information in a dream, and the chief butler suddenly remembered Joseph. He felt sorry about forgetting Joseph and told Pharaoh, **I do remember my faults this day** (Gen. 41:9).

Joseph was "hastily" pulled out of the dungeon and cleaned up to appear before the ruler of all Egypt. There, he interpreted Pharaoh's dream as seven good years to be followed by seven lean years. Joseph's "harvest" was to be given headship over the whole land next to Pharaoh and the responsibility for carrying out the plan to save all the surplus during the first seven years to hand out during the last seven.

If Joseph had not maintained a close fellowship with God all of those years, his "sickle" would not have been ready when the harvest was ready. Suppose he had become discouraged, given in to depression and fear, and given up on God, believing God had forsaken him? Would he ever have gotten out of prison?

In prison, Joseph undoubtedly died to self.

Who Do You Owe for Your Life?

We see another principle of sowing and reaping in the years of famine when the people of Egypt had given up all of their money, their animals, their land, and finally, were ready to become slaves of Pharaoh in order to have something to eat.

When they did this, Joseph said, "Okay, here is seed for you to sow the land. When the increase begins to come again, you keep four-fifths for yourself for *seed* for the next crop and for food. The other fifth (twenty percent) belongs to Pharaoh." (Gen. 47:23,24.)

I have always felt that a tenth for God was not enough. It seems to me that if Pharaoh should have twenty percent, then God should have at least that much. Most Christians will not even give the tithe.

I used to say things like, "Why should I tithe when my children need shoes? I can't even put groceries on the table right now. I am a grown man working as a foreman at a steel company, and I can't even buy groceries. Writing out a check to the church doesn't make sense!"

I regret that someone back then did not take the time to tell me about sickles, about strategy, insight, and cultivation, and about standing when you have done all you can.

This story of Pharaoh, Joseph, and the Egyptians makes a picture of how we are to be with God. Most of us operate in God one day and the next not. How in the world is He going to give us seed?

We should die to self and say to God, "As far as I am concerned, I am Yours."

Then God will say, "Fine. You have given Me everything. Here is a bag of seed."

His bag of seed is the Word, and the first thing you need to do is sow it in your land. Sow into the lives of other people. Sow into the ministries witnessed to you by the Holy Spirit.

The Egyptians who were fed by Pharaoh because of Joseph's insight from God said, "You have saved our lives, let us find favor in the sight of my lord, and we will be Pharaoh's slaves." (Gen. 47:25.)

How much more should someone saved by God from eternal damnation say, "You have saved my life. Let me be Your slave?"

You may wonder what being a slave of God means. It means doing what He tells you when He tells you and how He tells you. If you do this, you will walk in divine order, and your dream or vision will come to pass.

Become a Joseph by beginning to sow wherever you are:

- Get ten dollars worth of quarters from the bank, if you have little money, and begin to sow a quarter at a time.

- Go clean someone's house.

- Go change the oil in someone's car.

- Offer to babysit with someone else's child so that woman can get a little extra rest.

There are any number of ways you can find to sow that will bring you a harvest when you believe God for the increase. Cultivate someone else's garden while you plan your own strategy.

In the next chapter, we will be taking a more in-depth look at dreams and your destiny. After that, we are going to take a look at the other parts of the acronym which the Lord showed me out of *sickle*. They are kinetics, love, and endurance, or standing when you have done all, to stand.

4
Dreams Produce Destiny

And Joseph dreamed a dream, and he told it his brethren: and they hated him yet the more.

And he said unto them, Hear, I pray you, this dream which I have dreamed.

Genesis 37:5,6

To get an understanding of how dreams can produce destiny, we must take a look at how Joseph's destiny began.

I warn you, ahead of time, that when you get a dream or a vision, you are in trouble. Most people do not like visionaries.

If you are in trouble, your marriage is falling apart, you are an alcoholic and in and out of jail, your family can tolerate that most of the time. However, just get saved, go to church, get filled with the Holy Spirit, get your life back together, get your marriage straightened out, go to work and start giving money to the church — and your family and friends get upset!

They begin to wonder, "Is he involved with a cult? Is he giving away all his money to the church? That is wrong! He is in trouble. We had better do something."

They did not worry about how much you spent every week on alcohol or drugs, but when you start giving into the church, suddenly they want to know where your money is going. That is because they do not understand God, the Kingdom of God, or planting seed.

Genesis 37:5 says, "Then Joseph had a dream."

In the Hebrew, *dream* could mean vision, impression, or a literal night dream. Whatever he had, when he told his brothers, it did not make them happy! The Bible says they hated him even more. Is that not amazing?

You may have been out of high school for ten or twelve years, thinking that by the time you were thirty, you would have plenty of money. Now you are thirty and have found out that you should have gone to college.

So you think, "I'll enroll at night school, then get a degree from the university through continuing education classes. I can do that right here while I am working. I need to improve my mind and the quality of my life."

You begin to talk about this to people and some will say, "I don't like that guy. Why can't he just be a worker like us? Who does he think he is? He thinks he is better than us."

Joseph was only seventeen years old, and he was his father's favorite. He was the first son of Rachel, the only one of Jacob's four wives whom he had loved. Jacob worked fourteen years for his uncle in order to get Rachel as his wife. Joseph was the fruit of all of that labor, once his mother died.

But it was not being his father's favorite son, next to his younger brother Benjamin, which brought such a tremendous harvest for Joseph. He had a vision from God, a seed sowed into him by the Lord, and he chose to believe God and follow Him even in the midst of trials and tribulations.

Joseph's brothers did not have a vision. On the one hand, they did not have the trouble and persecution which Joseph had. One the other hand, they would have died of starvation if Joseph had not had a vision. They never sowed into his vision, and none of the brothers ever had one of his own, as far as we are told in the Bible. Yet they benefited from his.

On April 21, 1974, God placed a seed in me. From then, the time I was saved, there were always those "birds with long beaks" trying to steal that seed. The cares of life, discouragements and disappointments, and temptations of carnality tried to choke out the growth.

When you get a vision, you find yourself in a fight of faith. As long as I have faith in the seed, it will grow and do what it is destined to do. It matures by itself, Paul wrote.

Today, I preach to thousands. I have sowed the Word of God into thousands in Russia twice, once with more than four thousand people out of a crowd of five thousand responding to a call to give their hearts to Jesus. It looked like an avalanche moving toward the front! It was wonderful.

But that did not happen easily or quickly. If you get a vision from God and follow it, you will have truckloads of manure dropped at your door. But without it, you will never get a harvest. Only people with a vision are taken through a pit (tested on love), Potiphar's house (tested on obedience), and prison (tested on endurance) before they get to the palace.

The reason for all of the testing is that, without it to exercise your faith, obedience, and endurance, you will lose the vision or you will "blow it" when you get it.

A Lack of Vision Results in Dysfunction

God has saved us and put a vision of greatness in Christians today, I believe. He did this to save and preserve a generation out there dying, who are looking for a barn with seed in it to feed them.

I believe God said to Himself, "I have to raise up a Joseph generation. I have to raise up a visionary people who will run with the vision and stand through hardships to see it fulfilled. I must have a generation who will love one another and sow into one another's dream."

There are many dysfunctional people out there. There are many "co-dependent" people. But God did not call us to be dysfunctional. He did not call the Church to be dysfunctional. Perhaps you came to Christ dysfunctional, but He does not intend for you to stay that way. That's why He plants dreams or visions in us as seed for His harvests.

Once people become born again, they no longer should be dysfunctional. They have the seeds of function. We should be teaching them how to use those seeds, how to multiply them, and how to prosper.

The first thing his brothers did to Joseph was try to steal his identity. When you get a dream, the first thing that will happen to you is that people around will try to steal your identity as a Christian. Once you become born again, you have a new "blood" family. Your identity is "child of God," "citizen of the Kingdom of God," and "joint-heir with Jesus." That is your new, eternal identity.

One day, Joseph's brothers said, "Let's take his multicolored coat. It bothers us. Our robes are drab — gray, brown, or black, all one color. And here comes Joseph with all of these great colors."

So they stripped him of his tunic, but they could not strip him of his vision. They could not take away the dreams he had.

You may have been stripped externally, *but no human being can strip you internally*. Only you can give up on your dream.

You can hold on to that truth. No matter what trial you go through, no matter what temptation you face, no matter how many multicolored coats are stripped from you, no one but you can touch that seed. Your heart and vision will remain intact, if you cultivate faith and walk in love.

How many babies were slaughtered at the time of Moses?

How many babies were killed in Bethlehem when Jesus was a baby?

How many babies are being slaughtered today around the world through abortion?

The devil hates seed of any kind. He will go to any extent to kill and destroy something God has planted. But notice that Moses was preserved, Jesus was preserved, and God will preserve those who carry His vision.

The vision placed in Jesus helped Him endure the sufferings of the cross. In fact, He counted all of that as *joy*, because He had His eyes on the harvest, the outcome of the testings and trials. (Heb. 12:2.)

He hung on the cross, also stripped of His robe like Joseph. But they were not able to strip Him of His vision, which was being the firstfruits of those raised from the dead (1 Cor. 15:23) and the firstborn of many brethren. (Rom. 8:29.)

I heard a story about three people on a raft, survivors of some disaster. One was a physically incapacitated woman, who was pregnant. The second was a guy feverishly trying to preserve all of their lives. He caught fish with his hands, rigged up an awning to keep off the sun and rain, and wrung water out of his shirt into a cup to get fresh water for them to drink.

Then there was a third man who was lying in a fetal position along the side of the raft. When they asked him to help he would say, "What's the use? We're all going to die anyway."

To me, that is kind of a picture of the Church: Some are hurt and sick; and, others have given up and are just apathetically sitting in the services saying, "What's the use? The world's going to hell anyway." And there is the minority trying desperately to keep everyone alive.

The only time you hear even a grunt from the second kind of Christian is when you catch a fish or wring out some water. Then they raise up and want a bite or a drink. Afterwards, they go back to sleep.

God is much more patient than I am, and it is a good thing for all of us. If it were up to me, I would kick them out of the boat. I would tell them, if they did not help, "Over the side you go." But God is not like that. He knows each of us has a seed inside, and He will nurture that as long as He can.

The person working feverishly, however, is the one who will reach the palace. He is cultivating his seed by helping others. He has insight into preservation. He has a strategy for life and a vision.

Do not let go of your vision!

Your dream will affect your life. It is what moves you toward your destiny in God. Without a dream, you will never move toward destiny, much less fulfill it.

If you have a vision to follow, you will not horde your seed, nor will you eat it all up leaving none to plant.

Many churches and denominations have become ingrown. If others are not stamped with our particular persuasion, we will give them no money, no time, and are suspicious of their motives as well as their beliefs.

Do you realize what that has done? It has cut off our own harvests, our own growth. We have limited our growth and delayed our harvests. Believe me, it is more fun to give money away. It is more fun to invest it in other people. It is more fun to bless someone than to feel superior because we have money and they do not.

You Cannot Lose Unless You Give Up

It may have looked as if Joseph was a loser — hated by his brothers, thrown in a pit, thrown in prison for doing the "right thing," and seemingly forgotten. However, all of the time, God was elevating him. When God sees seed in you and vision in you, you will always come out on top.

Do not look at your precious coat being stripped off and disappearing into the hands of others.

Get your eyes back on your seed and say, "That was just a coat. I still have my vision from God."

Just because you have been talked about and even falsely accused, do not get embittered. Sow more seed. Do not get your eyes on your circumstances. Do not let your seed die. Envision it, speak to it, cultivate it, begin to see it grow. Whatever your circumstances, your vision always will pull you through.

When the butler forgot him as soon as he was reinstated in the palace, Joseph had a choice.

He could have said, "God, I can't believe this! I sowed into his life, and nothing is happening. I did what You told me, and now, he has forgotten all about me."

That is how the devil talks Christians into giving up, leaving the church, and even returning into the carnality of "Egypt." Joseph never gave up on God, even when he was betrayed, falsely accused, and forgotten.

Look what he said to Pharaoh when he did get into the palace and look what he did not say.

He did not go in there and say, "Man, I want you to know something. I almost missed giving you this interpretation because your cupbearer forgot me in prison."

He did not tell Pharaoh all about the great dream he had as a seventeen year old and all of the persecution it had cost him. He did not tell Pharaoh and the royal court what a wonderful seer he was. In fact, he did not build himself up at all. Here is what he said when Pharaoh asked if he could interpret the dream.

> And Joseph answered Pharaoh, saying, It is not in me: God shall give Pharaoh an answer of peace.
>
> And Joseph said unto Pharaoh, The dream of Pharaoh is one (the two dreams have the same meaning): God hath shewed Pharaoh what he is about to do.
>
> **Genesis 41:16,25**

"I cannot do anything," Joseph said. "God will do it."

He only told Pharaoh about God's revelation, about God's power to reveal the meaning of dreams, and about God's wisdom in telling them what to do about the hard times coming.

Vision will pull you to destiny. It did Joseph. Once you get a vision from God, you are on your way to greatness. You are on your way to conquering. That vision is a seed that *will* culminate in a harvest — if you do not give up. In Christ, you cannot lose unless you quit.

The reason is that Christ in you is the Conqueror. He is the victorious One; He is the authoritative One. And, if Christ is in you, then you can look forward to living on the level of life that He has set for you. The Church is to be a lifeboat, not a death boat.

You may be in a pit, you may be in prison, you may be alienated from family and feeling forsaken.

You may be imprisoned by a habit — drinking, lying, or maybe bad thoughts.

You may have been falsely accused, forgotten, and abandoned by others.

But if you belong to Jesus and you will not become embittered, you will come out a winner. When you have a vision, it has a way of bringing you to the top. I am not saying you will not have difficulties and problems. The point is that a vision or dream from God for your destiny is like being attached to a lifebuoy.

The vision can be pushed down temporarily, but it will float right back up bringing you with it. You may feel forsaken in the middle of an ocean of problems, but you will soon find yourself floating on your back, perhaps spitting out water but enjoying the sunshine.

Keep your eyes on Jesus, the Seed that is in you, and the vision He has given you will be fulfilled. We are of incorruptible seed, not corruptible.

> **Being born again, not of corruptible seed, but of incorruptible, by the word of God, which liveth and abideth for ever.**
>
> **1 Peter 1:23**

The Amplified Bible says:

> **You have been regenerated — born again — not from a mortal origin (seed, sperm) but from one that is immortal by the ever living and lasting Word of God.**

If you get your eyes off Jesus, your faith off the Seed, and begin to put your hand on circumstances, your vision could be destroyed. Joseph could have missed his destiny at any point along the path from his father's tent to Pharaoh's palace. Every trial was a point of testing for him, and by his choices to stay with the dream and follow God, he became stronger, not weaker.

Like Joseph, we need to be preparing barns for the harvest God is getting ready to bring in. He is allowing the people to become hungry in this country. We are into a time of famine for the Word of God, but there is coming a generation that will be hunting for spiritual food. If there are no barns, the harvest will rot in the fields.

God's people are to be "salt and light," a preserving element in the earth.

> **Ye are the salt of the earth: but if the salt have lost his savour, wherewith shall it be salted? it is**

> thenceforth good for nothing, but to be cast out, and to be trodden under foot of men.
>
> Ye are the light of the world. A city that is set on an hill cannot be hid.
>
> Neither do men light a candle, and put it under a bushel, but on a candlestick; and it giveth light unto all that are in the house.
>
> Let your light so shine before men, that they may see your good works, and glorify your Father which is in heaven.
>
> Matthew 5:13-16

That is God's vision for the Church, and His visions never fail. A revival is coming, and there will be some churches ready, but not all. Even in Jesus' day, He said the harvest was plentiful, but the workers were few.

> Then saith he unto his disciples, The harvest truly is plenteous, but the labourers are few;
>
> Pray ye therefore the Lord of the harvest, that he will send forth labourers into his harvest.
>
> Matthew 9:37,38

It is time that more Christians begin to develop the mentality that the Church is going to get bigger and better, not weaker and defeated.

It is time we began to sow seeds such as "God wants to make us the head and not the tail." (Deut. 28:13.)

We need the "k" in *sickle* — kinetic energy. We need determination and strength, because we have all been lazy about the things of God.

5

Kinetics: Energy in Motion

He was in the world, and the world was made by him, and the world knew him not.

He came unto his own, and his own received him not.

But as many as received him, to them gave he power to become the sons of God, even to them that believe on his name.

John 1:10-12

There are two things science says cannot be created and cannot be destroyed. These two things have always been, scientists say. One is *mass*, and the other is *energy*.

We are not concerned in this book with mass. However, energy can be:

- Altered in different ways
- Converted into different forms
- But not destroyed

Now think about John 1:1:

In the beginning was the Word, and the Word was with God, and the Word *was* God.

And Genesis 1:1 says:

In the beginning God created the heaven and the earth.

God, being energy, has always been in existence.

God, being the original mass, has always been in existence.

God was not created, yet through His energy, all things were created.

God appeared on earth in the form of His only begotten Son, Jesus Christ. (John 3:16.) Some prophecies about Jesus reveal Him as "God's arm," His power in the earthly realm.

> **And He saw that there was no man, and wondered that there was no intercessor [no one to intervene on behalf of truth and right]:** *therefore His own* **arm brought Him victory, and His righteousness [having the Spirit without measure] sustained him. [1 John 2:1,2; Isa. 53:11; Col. 2:9.]**
>
> **Isaiah 59:16** AMP

God created man, a spirit being, in His image (Gen. 1:26), therefore man *will* always be in existence. The only question is, where will he exist after he leaves earth: Heaven or Hell?

The word for the energy possessed by a body (a mass) because of its motion is *kinetic*. Other definitions, or synonyms, for *kinetic* are:

Of, relating to, or produced by motion; possessing, exerting, or displaying energy; active, vigorous, dynamic, forceful, and energetic.

From this, you can see that Christians need to get their mass in motion, to become energetic, forceful, and active in sowing the Seed into their own lives and into the world. The state of America today reflects the state of the Church — inactive, passive, not displaying energy through motion. And the enemy is filling the vacuum in society left by the lack of motion of the Church with wickedness, crime, and poverty.

We already have learned that Christ is the Seed planted in us and, as the written Word, the seed we plant in all areas of our lives. In the verses at the beginning of this chapter, John wrote that "to as many as received" Jesus, He "gave the power to become sons of God." (v. 12.)

If you believe on His name, you already have received *power* to move you into the position of sonship. *The Seed is the force behind the motion.*

The energy provided by water falling over a dam will turn a turbine, through which that energy can be altered into electricity. That is *kinetic*. But there is a force behind the energy, and that is called *gravity*.

Gravity creates the motion that produces the kinetic energy that is altered into electricty.

But what good is the energy created by the motion of that waterfall instigated by the force called gravity *unless it is captured* as electricity. A waterfall is beautiful, but it is of no practical good unless the energy is harnessed.

The Body of Christ is not capturing or harnessing the force — the energy — the power of God — to move us out of our predicaments in life, out of the attitude of defeatism or escapism, and into victory.

In the times that lie ahead, we must understand this whole concept of sickles, including the "k" for kinetics. Christians have not been "neutered," although many times we feel and act as though we had. We are part of the gears of the operation of the Godhead, which existed from before the foundation of the world and can literally move Heaven and earth.

Christ: the Force Behind the Motion

The Seed of God is the power of God, and Christ in you is the hope of the manifestation of the presence of Almighty God in this generation. Christ in you is the hope of glory. (Col. 1:27.) He is the Seed, or the force behind the motion, that creates power to be converted from an "old man" to a new one.

And in the new man, God is present as the Holy Spirit to convert spiritual energy into tangible form as signs and wonders. We are led by the Spirit from a natural, carnal state and appetite to maturity (perfection) in Jesus. (Eph. 4:13.) But it is the power of Christ that causes the motion, which is transformed or converted into supernatural changes and demonstrations.

God was saying, "To impoverished, sick, and unrighteousness man, I will give you Seed that can be planted in your spirits and into your lives to transform you into new creatures (2 Cor. 5:17), that no longer are fallen and in bondage to Satan. All you have to do is receive this Seed and let it work in your lives."

He first promised this to Adam and Eve as they were being exiled from the Garden of Eden.

By receiving that Seed, I can have the motion to convert God's will, purpose, and plan into tangible results — the power of God in my life. Now I can move that which was stuck.

I once had a mind that could not get rid of ill thoughts about others; now, I have the Seed in me that provides the force to create motion and energy for my mind to be renewed. The kinetic energy provided by that force in motion has converted my thoughts. Now I think good thoughts about others. Now my words are powerful.

The energy of the tongue in motion has been converted from death to life. (Prov. 18:21.) Yours can be transformed the same way. James said no man is able to tame the tongue, "an unruly member" of the body. (James 3:8.) However, the Holy Spirit can transform the tongue.

The Holy Spirit can go where we cannot, and He has the knowledge that we do not have in order to enable us to do what we ordinarily could not do. The Holy Spirit knows where to apply the energy gained by the force of the Seed in motion in our lives.

Another example is the kinetic energy of drugs in the body of a person who is sick or injured.

When a doctor diagnoses your problem, he administers — or prescribes to be administered — a certain medication. That medication, whether taken orally or by injection, has a force that causes it to find its way to the right area, where it begins to create the motion that will provide energy to transform the sick or injured part of the body into health.

However, the waterfall is no good to us, no matter how much energy the force of gravity produces, unless it is used, and the medicine is no good to us sitting in the bottle. Likewise, the power of God is no good to us unless it is used to transform our lives and society.

God created us with the right to choose, so He will not force us to do the things we should do. It is not enough simply to accept the Seed and have eternal life with the Father. We are told to "put off the old and put on the new," to change our attitudes, habits, and behaviors to fit the new creature made in the image of Christ. (2 Cor. 5:17; Eph. 4:24.)

How can we do that without using the power of the Holy Spirit? Jesus said that without the Father, He could do nothing. Likewise, in ourselves, we can do nothing. (John 5:19.) Jesus, while on earth, allowed Himself to be a "turbine" through which the power of God flowed to people.

How can we "occupy" victoriously until Jesus returns, without making use of the power of the Holy Spirit?

Perhaps the most priceless thing in the world today is *energy*: oil, coal, electric, nuclear. Without energy for fuel, the world's systems would run down and people would die by the millions. Everything would grind to a halt, because we do not operate by horse and buggy any longer. Without the spiritual energy that should be flowing through the power plant of the Church, times are waxing worse and worse.

The Church has access to all of the energy needed, and we are not using it. All of those who are truly born again have the Holy Spirit living in their spirits. Many Christians have the Holy Spirit manifesting in the fullness of the baptism. But to most believers, He is like "water pouring over the edge of the dam" with all of the energy dissipating in the air.

We look at that "Water" and think, "Man, if we could just do . . . Something ought to be going on . . . What happened to all of the revivals and miracles of the past? We ought to be able to move in that today."

Others keep preaching that the power is coming, and the time is near when the power of the Holy Spirit will be poured out into vessels for use again. But it will not, if we do not understand how to cooperate with Him in making a way for this to happen.

We have the power of God resident within us to provide motion for energy, but we do not cooperate.

Look at Genesis 1:2:

And the earth was without form, and void; and darkness was upon the face of the deep. And the Spirit of God moved (hovered) **upon the face of the waters.**

In Hebrew, the word translated *moved* means "fluttered." So the Holy Spirit was fluttering over a formless mass void (empty) of life. The mass existed without form and was covered by darkness. Why was the Holy Spirit "fluttering" over it? He was there because *He is the force that puts energy in motion.* He was the power that converted the mass into a different form: the planet earth.

It will do us no good to understand kinetic energy, which is formed by the mass of a body in motion, if we cannot use that understanding in a practical way.

It will do us no good to understand that the Holy Spirit is the force behind all motion that creates energy — spiritual and natural — if we do not understand how that applies to us personally. We must understand how to allow Him to operate His force (power) in our lives. So how do we do that? We become "turbines" for God.

We Are "Turbines" in the Kingdom

In every area where I am not living as a son of God, there is an illegal trespass by my carnal nature under the influence of the god of this world. (2 Cor. 4:4.) In those areas, I am devoid of power to change my life or to help change the lives of people around me. Yet, I am walking around with the Great Power of the universe inside me.

Each born-again person has been made into a "turbine" for the use of the Master. You can sit back and watch the waterfall and wish. You can hope that someday someone will come along and somehow cause the turbine to work — but no one will. *You have to choose to work.* I have to do it myself. Each church or ministry has to become working turbines.

A *turbine* in Biblical terms is a "vessel" for conducting the Holy Spirit's power where it is needed.

> **But we have this treasure in earthen vessels, that the excellency of the *power* may be of God, and not of us.**
>
> **2 Corinthians 4:7**

In corporate unity, what happens is that enough individual turbines are working together producing spiritual motion that provides kinetic energy from the force in us, the Holy Spirit. A popular movie some years ago had an occult energy available called "the force." That was an attempt to display a counterfeit of the power of the Holy Spirit.

The Godhead — Father, Son, and Holy Spirit — is the real *Force* behind everything. When the power of the Holy Spirit is manifested in our services, we call it "the anointing." If the people of God would come together in unity — not uniformity — there is nothing in existence that could stop the Word of God.

Jesus showed us an example, even before He died, rose again, and sent the Holy Spirit to live in us. In Luke 9:1, He called the disciples together and gave them "power and authority." The Greek word is *exousia*, which is a derivative of *dunamis*, meaning "miraculous power."

He gave them power to heal diseases, and authority over all demons. Jesus was training them to become *working turbines* that would allow the power of the Holy Spirit, power to transform lives and heal bodies, to pour through them to other people.

When He gave the disciples the promise of the Holy Spirit, He said:

> **But ye shall receive power, after that the Holy Ghost is come upon you: and ye shall be witnesses unto me both in Jerusalem, and in all Judaea, and in Samaria, and unto the uttermost part of the earth.**
>
> **Acts 1:8**

He was saying, "You will demonstrate for Me with signs and wonders what a waterfall can do in a life if it is allowed to operate through a turbine. You can show Christians that they can light up a whole city. They can warm a family in the coldness of a night during the storms of life. They can transform an individual from one frozen by darkness to one warmed by the Son. But they cannot do this without becoming 'working turbines' to carry the Power to those people."

The Church has access to the most precious commodity known to man — energy to transform everything — but we walk right by it looking for the energy of this world.

The Apostle Paul, one of the greatest "turbines" who ever lived, wrote much about this concept:

> **And my speech and my preaching was not with enticing words of man's wisdom, but in demonstration of the Spirit and *of power*.**
>
> **1 Corinthians 2:4**

> **For the kingdom of God is not in word, but *in power*.**
>
> **1 Corinthians 4:20**

He wrote more than two dozen times of the power of God and how we have access to that power. He did not just sit and look at the energy created by gravity pushing water over the falls and *wish* that he could use it. He used it.

While studying on understanding seed from planting to harvest, I ran across a verse in Paul's second letter to Timothy talking about conditions in the "perilous times" of the last days, and a "light" came on in my mind.

> **Having a form of godliness, but** *denying the power* **thereof: from such turn away.**
>
> 2 Timothy 3:5

What does it mean to deny the power of God? It means that, instead of allowing Him to use you to carry His power to others, you sit and watch the waterfall. Christians are the only means that God has chosen for the Holy Spirit to flow through to convert His power into tangible demonstrations to the world of a new life in Christ.

How To Become a Working Turbine

I think it is easy to see that we *are* turbines, or vessels, designed to cooperate with God in carrying the power of the Holy Spirit to others. The kinetic spiritual energy caused by the force of the Holy Spirit pouring His living water through us can become enough power to change the world.

If you understand anything about turbines, you know that they must be clean and in good working order before they can be efficiently used. Instead of being "clean" vessels, much of the Church today seems to fit Paul's description of mankind in the "last days."

His descriptions ought to be of carnal, worldly people, those without God. Yet we see people in the Church who are lovers of themselves and proud, lovers of pleasure more than God, and having a form of godliness but denying there is any power in God for today. (2 Tim. 3:1-8.)

In nearly every local church today, there are those who are unloving, arrogant, disobedient, and malicious gossips. Charles Colson in his book *The Body*, writes about two deacons who began a fist fight in church with one another.

I have met some brutal Christians. They have no regard for your feelings. They only want to pull down, not build up. This is why the laborers to work in the harvest are few. Few people are willing to adjust their lives, to change their ways, in order to be pure vessels for the Lord's use.

Too many of us think *we* are the *treasure*. We do not see ourselves simply as vessels to carry the Lord where He wants to go and to cooperate with Him in doing His thing, not our own. Jesus said, "Not My will, but Thine be done." (Matt. 26:39,42.) And too many are not willing to do that.

The Church needs to be like Samson, asking for the Spirit to come upon us mightily. (Judg. 15:14.) When we ask for the wind of the Holy Spirit to move, we are asking for energy to be released in the people of God. We are asking that Christians begin to move, to provide the motion that creates energy to convert into tangible expression.

When the Spirit moved on Samson, strength came upon him. He was able to do what he ordinarily could not do. After his hair was cut, he no longer was a fit turbine for God to use. (Judg. 16:17.) It was not the loss of his *hair* that cost him, but what the hair represented — consecration and separation to the purpose of God, obedience to a vow made to God, and the submission of his will to the will of God. That also is the "secret" of the strength of any Christian.

When Samson woke up and found himself bound the final time, he said, "I'll just go out and shake myself free as I have before." (Judg. 16:20.)

His words show that some of those last-day characteristics had been allowed to develop in him — love of pleasure more than God, pride, and focus on himself:

• It never was Samson's own power and strength which did the great exploits.

• It always is God who shakes heaven and earth. (Hag. 2:6,21; Heb. 12:26.)

• It is His sovereign will that moves where He desires, and you and I have nothing to do with it, lest we forget who is Lord of the Church.

Someone may think he is the greatest evangelist of all time, but he had nothing to do with the converts coming in droves to the altars of his great crusade meetings. It was not his strength or power that did it, but the sovereign move of the Holy Spirit. However, that evangelist deserves credit for obedience, for saying "yes" to God, when He chose to use him as a "turbine" for His power.

> . . . **Not by might, nor by power, but by my spirit, saith the Lord of hosts.**
>
> **Zechariah 4:6**

Samson's eyes were gouged out, much like the Church today, without vision, without strategy, without insight, hoarding every dime that comes in and every person who comes into local churches.

We are trying to shake ourselves. We boast in our own accomplishments, while ridiculing others when they move in the Spirit of God.

The Philistines, Israel's enemies, laughed at Samson when he lost his power. They called for him to come and entertain them. (Judg. 16:25.)

The Church today is entertaining the world. We appear on secular talk shows as foolish, formless Christians, haters of others, lovers of self, and screaming prejudice against others. In the same breath, we proclaim to love God. And the world is entertained by us poor, powerless people.

A Turning of the Tide

My heart aches because of the hypocrisy that lives within the walls of the Kingdom of God. It bruises my heart daily as I think of the irrational statements and the self-serving agendas of some professing to know Christ, yet denying His power.

But I have news for the world: Our hair is beginning to grow. We are beginning to recognize how and where we fell.

And we are saying, "God, will You give us one more chance? One more sermon, God? Perhaps this night thousands will come to know You. Perhaps this night many will come up out of wheelchairs." We are beginning to say "yes" to God.

I do not have to worry about tomorrow, if I say "yes" to God in all areas of my life. If I wake up with a dilemma and do not understand what to do, my God understands, and He will make a way where there is no way. He knows all that I need to know.

The Church cannot bring in the harvest without a sharpened, ready sickle. The "sickle," as we have seen, includes strategy, insight or understanding of the Word, cultivation (serving others), and kinetic energy flowing through us as power from the Holy Spirit.

There are two other aspects of the sickle that will explain more about becoming the "working turbines" that God needs for the harvest: love and endurance. Without love, God cannot use you. If commitment, consecration, and santification make you a fit turbine, then love is the switch that allows the power to flow.

6

Love Turns On the Power

Such hope (of eternal salvation) **never disappoints or deludes or shames us, for God's love has been poured out in our hearts through the Holy Spirit Who has been given to us.**

But God shows and clearly proves His [own] love for us by the fact that while we were still sinners Christ, the Messiah, the Anointed One, died for us.
Romans 5:5,8 AMP

All of us would like the power of God to flow through us, I am sure. But there is a "switch" that puts that turbine to its proper use, something that determines whether the power is "off" or "on." In the Kingdom of God, that switch is *love*.

Paul wrote that the love of God has been poured out in our hearts by the Holy Spirit, and in Romans 8:1, he wrote that we are to live according to the dictates of the Spirit. We must understand the pouring out of God's love in order to live by His commandments, instructions, or "dictates."

The Holy Spirit filled up our reservoir with God for a purpose, when we received Christ in our hearts. Before we receive Christ, we are led by the soul — the mind, will, and emotions. But once we are new creatures, we are not to be led any longer by our souls. We are to be led by the Spirit witnessing to our spirits.

I follow the Spirit and the dictates of the Spirit, which is God's love. When I understand that God's love has been poured out in my thoughts, my feelings, and my intents, I comprehend Matthew 12:34 better.

> **O generation of vipers, how can ye, being evil, speak good things? for out of the abundance of the heart the mouth speaketh.**

The Amplified Bible translates it something like this, "You offspring of vipers. How can you speak good things when you are evil and wicked?"

We hear the last part of that verse quoted often, but we tend to forget about the first part which really gives us a better understanding.

Jesus was saying to them, "You who have been birthed from the seed of the carnal nature, how can you speak good things? Your 'reservoir' (heart, feelings, intents, emotions) has been filled with evil. And you speak out of the abundance of the overflow from this reservoir."

Why is that important for us to understand? It is important because the Word of God declares that, now that I have been filled with His love, I can utter words that will align myself with the will of God and not the will of evil.

If I am filled with the love of God, I should speak words of love. I can even speak unpleasant truths about or to someone — as long as I do it in love. First Peter 2:22 says that Jesus was guilty of no sin and deceit was not found on His lips.

But, you ask, what about the harsh words He spoke to the Pharisees? He even called them "snakes."

Speaking the truth is not sin when it is done according to the will of God and in love. Jesus was pronouncing judgment upon the Pharisees, His own to whom He came and was not received. (John 1:11.) He was speaking *facts*. It is when you backbite, gossip, or enjoy repeating even truths about other people that should not be told, that it becomes sin.

We know Jesus loved the people of His generation in Judea, because He mourned over them when He pronounced judgment. (Matt. 23:37.) He loved them and wanted to nurture them as a mother fowl gathers her brood under her wings — but they would not let Him.

When you speak words of hate, bitterness, resentment, or anger, the Father does not hear you. In other words, your prayers are to no avail.

> **And whenever you stand praying, if you have anything against any one, forgive him and let it drop — leave it, let it go — in order that your Father Who is in heaven may also forgive you your [own] failings and shortcomings and let them drop.**
>
> **But if you do not forgive, neither will your Father in heaven forgive your failings and shortcomings.**
>
> **Mark 11:25,26 AMP**

A Lack of Love Closes God's Ears

It is an incredible thought that many Christians have been in church, perhaps even working in some capacity, but God's ears have been plugged to them for years because of unforgiven grudges or offenses held against other people. The "electricity" of God's power has stopped flowing through them. The turbine is getting rusty.

The remedy is to *forgive* and *be forgiven*, then choose to begin to walk in love with everyone. *Love is a choice, not an emotion*, and in the Kingdom of God, it is not an option but a commandment. Choose to love, and the emotion will follow. That good feeling follows the choice to love; it is not the instigator of love.

If you do not believe that love is important, look at John 3:16:

> **For God so loved the world, that he gave his only begotten Son, that whosoever believeth in him should not perish, but have everlasting life.**

The entire plan of redemption came out of love. In fact, the Bible says that God *is* love (1 John 4:16), not that He *has* love. Love is the essence of God's character, nature, and ways. There is no way we cannot receive His love in us when we receive Jesus.

Jesus told His disciples that the one way the world would know for sure that He was God and would follow Him was not signs and wonders, as we sometimes think. It was for the world to see how much the followers of Jesus *loved* one another.

> **A new commandment I give unto you, That ye love one another; as I have loved you, that ye also love one another.**
>
> **By this shall all men know that ye are my disciples, if ye have love one to another.**
>
> **John 13:34,35**

In the Old Testament, God's people were commanded to obey; in the New, we are commanded to *love* and *obey*. And love is the one characteristic that Jesus said would cause the world to know that we are His people.

Other religions have good moral standards, good ethics, and do good deeds. Only Christianity stresses love for your neighbor as well as love of God.

Other religions fear their gods. Only Christianity *loves* God and teaches that God loves us. Jesus also said that He loved us just as the Father does.

> **As the Father hath loved me, so have I loved you: continue ye in my love.**
>
> **John 15:9**

When we do not love, we are polluting our own bodies and our own lives. It does not matter who has done what to you; it does not matter who has talked about you. If you want to have a healthy physical and spiritual life, *do not answer back*. And, above all, do not judge or hold grudges.

The Bible says to pray for those who persecute you. (Matt. 5:44.) That is walking the love walk.

A Lack of Love Is Spiritual Pollution

Instead of loving a fellow child of God as they love themselves (John 13:34), some Christians not only judge others and harbor judgments against others, but actually are praying destruction onto one another!

I know some who pray, "Oh, God, just expose So-and-so. Father, show them up for the creeps they are. Pull down that ministry. *I* don't like it. I don't think it is right."

That is "witchcraft" prayers and assuming the role of God.

Some Christians get sick, have their finances attacked, and perhaps even die prematurely, but seem to have no idea that it is because they are not walking in love. Their thoughts and words pollute their lives and deprive their bodies of health.

We have a lot of Christians walking around destroyed, walking through life, going through the motions but never coming to a place of fulfillment.

Then they say, "Well, God's Word doesn't work. He doesn't heal today. He doesn't provide for us today. He doesn't operate in power today. I guess that really was just for the early Church."

A lack of love means the love of God within you is dammed up by some barrier in your heart and cannot flow forth. What is not released turns sour and bitter and becomes poison. Then, when the poison grows, it usually is released through the tongue.

Where there is no love, evil thoughts and words come to fill up the heart. James wrote about this condition, basing his warnings on Proverbs 18:21, which says that "life and death" are in the power of the tongue. So the tongue has power.

> **And the tongue [is] a fire. [The tongue is a] world of wickedness set among our members, contaminating and depraving the whole body and setting on fire the wheel of birth — the cycle of man's nature — being itself ignited by hell (Gehenna)** (Gehenna is the lake of fire).
>
> **But the human tongue can be tamed by no man. It is (an undisciplined, irreconcilable) restless evil, full of death-bringing poison.**
>
> James 3:6,8 AMP

It would be profitable for all Christians who have a problem with wrong attitudes and unforgiveness to meditate on the entire third chapter of James. He shows very clearly how a lack of love means a fullness of poison.

The words we speak come out of the overflow of the heart and poisonous words hurt us as much as the people we speak against.

The Apostle Paul also wrote about this, in Ephesians 4:29. He wrote to "let no foul or polluting" words come out of our mouths.

When I began to pastor and saw how many people were sick, and when I saw that any time an invitation went out for healing the altars were lined, I did not understand it. I knew the Bible said that if His children heard and obeyed, He would put none of the diseases of "Egypt" on them.

> . . . **If thou wilt diligently hearken to the voice of the Lord thy God, and wilt do that which is right in his sight, and wilt give ear to his commandments, and keep all his statutes, I will put none of these diseases upon thee, which I have brought upon the Egyptians: for I am the Lord that healeth thee.**
> **Exodus 15:26**

I said, "God, how is it Your Word is not working?"

The Lord answered, "Because they do not understand the love walk."

Medical research says that eighty percent of all of the people who are sick have psychosomatic illnesses. That is not imaginary illnesses, but sickness and disease caused by thoughts and emotions, not physical causes.

Not long ago, I saw a medical doctor on a major network talk show who had spent the last twenty-three years studying the effects of prayer on hundreds of patients. He found that those who were prayed for more readily and quickly regained their health than those who were not.

And the healing was *not* psychosomatic, or by suggestion, because the people did not know that he was praying for them. As I understand it, the doctor was not even Christian, but he was speaking words of love and welfare over those people.

If you do not walk the love walk, I promise you that you will speak out poisonous words over your own life and the lives of others. Therefore, whatever a man sows, he will also reap. (Gal. 6:7.)

A Lack of Love Alters Your Destiny

In addition to contaminating your life and polluting your health, when you do not operate out of love, you "set on fire" God's plans for you.

Notice that James 3:6 in *The Amplified Bible* quoted above says that you "set on fire the wheel of birth." That means the course of your destiny, or "the cycle of your nature."

You set on fire God's plan for you, and it becomes hindered, destroyed, or altered by Satan.

My life had been set on fire. I had been altered by the sin nature from what God purposed me to be. But when I received Christ, He put out the fire and gave me a flame that cleanses but does not consume — the Holy Spirit. The reconstructive power of God took me out of an ash heap and gave me beauty for ashes. (Isa. 61:3.)

The Bible tells us to follow in the footsteps of Jesus, to be like Him. That is what "taking up your cross" means.

And He said to all, If any person wills to come after Me, let him deny himself — that is, disown himself, forget, lose sight of himself and his own interests, refuse and give up himself — and take up his cross daily, and follow Me [that is, cleave

**steadfastly to Me, conform wholly to My example, in
living and if need be in dying also].**

Luke 9:23 AMP

I used to think "bearing your cross" meant walking around defeated, beaten down, and suffering for Jesus. That does not bring Him any glory. *Denying yourself* means giving up your own way daily, giving up what you want for what He wants. If you do that, your soul and body *may* suffer, but it brings Him glory and brings you victory.

Denying yourself means not answering back, not hitting back, not retaliating for evil done to you — and not even resenting it!

Did Jesus deny Himself when He was reviled, beaten, and crucified? When His beard was plucked out by the roots? When a crown of long, sharp thorns was pushed down on His head?

Did He deny Himself when He said, "Not My will, but Thine be done"?

Did He deny Himself when He spent forty days fasting in the wilderness and then withstood temptations of Satan against His spirit, soul, and body?

Jesus fulfilled His destiny. Not one word proceeded out of His mouth that did not flow out of the love poured into Him by the Father.

The Apostle Peter wrote that our lives are to "set forth the wonderful deeds of Jesus and display His virtues and perfection," because He called us out of darkness into "marvelous light." (1 Pet. 2:9 AMP.)

Stephen, the first martyr in the Church, was such a working turbine that he made the Jews as angry at him as they had been at Jesus — perhaps even angrier, because they did not wait to let the Romans deal with Stephen. They took him out immediately and stoned him.

Read Acts 7, and you will see that every word Stephen spoke was in love, although the truth he spoke was not pleasant to his hearers. He followed the example of Jesus even unto his death. Acts 6:8 says that Stephen was "full of faith and power." His last words were not poisonous revilings on those who killed him. They were words of love and forgiveness. (Acts 7:60.)

My son came home from skating one night and brought one of those little tubes that glow. In the morning, it was still dark when I got up to wake him for school, and when I walked into his room, that little tube was over there on the dresser just glowing away.

And the Lord showed me that is the way we are, when we are working turbines. In the spiritual realm, we glow. The more we walk the love walk, the more we are like Him, the greater the glow.

Every person is a turbine of some sort, either pouring forth the love of God to others or pouring forth the poison of the enemy to others. Either way, we also affect ourselves and our own lives.

Love Is Necessary to Harvest

If you begin to try to walk the love walk, you can be sure that other people's poison will be turned on you. Misery loves company and usually resents happiness and joy.

Perhaps you have had poison poured out on you all of your childhood and younger days. God will clean that off if you take it to Him and forgive those who did it. Let go of the poisonous words that said you were ugly, too fat or too thin, dumb and stupid, or never able to learn or do anything right.

God knew you before the foundation of the world (Matt. 25:34), and He chose you before you ever chose Him. (Mark 13:20; John 15:16.) The Holy Spirit sought you and kept after you until you surrendered. Would He have done that if you were not worth it? Forget those lies and believe what God said about you.

You are not just an accident, or a warm body filling a seat in church. You have a purpose in life. God has a destiny for you. Seek the dream He has for your life and cling to it like that buoy that we spoke of earlier.

As a Church, the Body of Christ is "a chosen generation," "a royal priesthood" and "an holy nation." (1 Pet. 2:9.) We were chosen to sow seeds and reap harvests for God.

Without love, the power will not flow, and the harvest will not be gathered in. The power will be there, but the switch is off. Your love walk is birthed out of the love of God which was shed abroad in your heart by the Holy Spirit. (Rom. 5:5.) But you must *choose* whether to let go of those things which block His love from flowing. That is why love is a choice.

If you speak nothing but love, then you have turned the turbine of your will to "on."

How do we maintain the love walk? We do that by allowing the Lord to fulfill His Word to "establish us."

Now to him (be glory) **that is of power to stablish you according to my gospel, and the preaching of Jesus Christ, according to the revelation of the mystery, which was kept secret since the world began.**

Romans 16:25

Paul also wrote that God not only began the work in you, but that He will finish it — if you allow Him. You always have a choice to receive the work of God in your life.

> **Being confident of this very thing, that he which hath begun a good work in you will perform it until the day of Jesus Christ.**
>
> **Philippians 1:6**

The best sermon is a life lived before nonbelievers that shows forth the love of God for them. When you become born again, your mass is converted into a different form, a new creature. If you truly have become a new creature, that Seed which God has planted in you will begin to grow and change and transform your outer nature and your life. Your lifestyle will reflect the inner transformation.

If there is no power of conversion visible in tangible form, you *might* be a Christian, but you are not in obedience to God. You are not witnessing for Him by allowing His love to flow through you. And your *sickle*, the spiritual traits that enable you to glean in the harvest, is damaged.

You see, the *love walk* is the "bottom-line" law of God. It is *the Royal Law of the Kingdom.*

7

The Love Walk: The Royal Law

> And He replied to him, You shall love the Lord your God with all your heart, and with all your soul, and with all your mind (intellect). [Deut. 6:5.]
>
> This is the great (most important, principal) and first commandment.
>
> And a second is like it, You shall love your neighbor as [you do] yourself. [Lev. 19:18.]
>
> These two commandments sum up and upon them depends all the Law and the prophets.
>
> Matthew 22:37-40 AMP

We know that loving God first and our neighbors as ourselves second were two of the original Ten Commandments, but how do we know that is the foundation law or "the Royal Law" of the Kingdom of God?

We know this because James wrote it in the New Testament.

> If indeed you [really] fulfill *the royal Law*, in accordance with the Scripture, You shall love your neighbor as [you love] yourself, you do well. [Lev. 19:18.]
>
> James 2:8 AMP

Royal law is loving God with all your heart, your soul, your might, and your strength, and then loving

your neighbor as you do yourself. If you will understand this concept and begin to operate in it, you will
see the destiny of the Lord for you begin to surface.

You are not an afterthought of God. He has plans
for you.

A little Hispanic woman was fulfilling God's plan
for her and for me when she came up to me in 1974,
handed me a tract, and said, "Do you know Jesus?"
God spoke to her by His Spirit to do that. He knew
it was going to happen even from the foundation of
the world.

I believe He told the angels, "Get ready! That hard-
headed, good-for-nothing drunkard of a man, that
angry Louis Kayatin, is about to get born again."

I left that service thinking everyone there was
weird, but I had something in my hand that eventually
burned into my heart.

On the back of that little tract, it simply said, "Pray,
and ask God to forgive you of your sins. Ask Him into
your heart, and you will be a new person."

At the time, I worked the night shift, and for that
entire shift that night, I prayed that prayer perhaps a
hundred times. And I felt so good! I walked through
the smoke and fire of that old coke and steel plant with
all kinds of problems, but my feet were about a foot
off the floor. Something had happened to me.

I had gotten hooked up with my destiny. God had
planted His Seed in my heart. The devil had tried to
send me to hell. He tried to browbeat me, work on me,
and entice me to make choices in agreement with the
lusts of the flesh. But God, in His mercy, sent the Lord
Jesus Christ two thousand years ago to die at Calvary
to save me.

The story of Jesus never gets old to me, for I know that is when God restored those who would accept redemption to the destiny He had planned for us before the foundation of the world.

Too many Christians today do not have any joy. They have little happiness and no peace, because they are not being fulfilled in their destinies. God restored their destinies, but they are not fulfilling them, because they do not know how to love. Instead of loving and building others up, they want to ridicule, criticize, and judge other Christians.

One way to maintain your peace and joy is not to hang around with those who do not have any!

Did you ever notice that eagles do not fly with sparrows? An eagle flies way above the other birds. If you want to fly with eagles, you need to go find an eagle. Pass up the crows and buzzards you have been hanging around with.

Those birds eat "dead meat." If you eat the right stuff — God's food — you will be able to fly with the eagles. You need fresh manna from the Word, not spoiled, rotten, recycled food.

I say to my people what John wrote to a certain Christian lady and her children whom he loved:

> **And now I beg you, lady (Cyria), not as if I were issuing a new charge (injunction or command), but [simply recalling to your mind] the one we have had from the beginning, that we love one another.**
> **2 John 5** AMP

How To Know That You Truly Love

How do you know that you really love God? Is it because you say so? Is it because you sing the loudest in praise and worship? No, you know by the fruits in your life. (Gal. 5:22,23.) John explained like this:

> And what this love consists in is this, that we live and walk in accordance with and guided by His commandments — His orders, ordinances, precepts, teaching. *This* is the commandment, as you have heard from the beginning, that you continue to walk in love — guided by it and following it.
>
> 2 John 6 AMP

"Oh, wait a minute," you may say. "Do you mean that to love my brother means just to do what God said? I thought to love my brother, I have to get goosebumps and bake him an apple pie, and tell him something I don't feel — like, 'I really like you.' "

That is not what God is saying. He is saying that you love your brother *and* you love Him when you do what He tells you to do. In the Bible, He already has told us what to do. If you are totally committed to God, then you cannot help but be rightly related to your brothers and sisters.

That is why John wrote that, if you hate your brother but say you love God, you are a liar. (1 John 4:20.) In fact, He made it stronger. He said, if you do that, *the truth is not in you!*

Love will guide you into the fulfillment of your destiny.

John also wrote about *how* to know that you are coming to know Him better.

> And this is how we may discern [daily by experience] that we are coming to know Him — to perceive, recognize, understand and become better acquainted with Him: if we keep (bear in mind, observe, practice) His teachings (precepts, commandments).
>
> 1 John 2:3 AMP

If you stop sinning, you can perceive that you are knowing Him better. That is how you measure your fellowship with Jesus: by how you observe His teachings. Perhaps you used to lie like a skunk, but now you do not lie anymore. You are getting to know God.

Do we know Him in this generation of the Church? Do we know who God is? How can we, when absolutes are rarely taught anymore? In public school, in the entertainment media, and in the news media, we are bombarded over and over with situational ethics: What is wrong in one situation is right in another.

John wrote about this kind of person:

> Whoever says, I know Him — I perceive, recognize, understand and am acquainted with Him — but fails to keep and obey His commandments (teachings) is a liar, and the Truth [of the Gospel] is not in him.
>
> 1 John 2:4 AMP

Most Christians would be highly offended if someone told them that the truth of the Gospel was not in them because they criticized other Christians, cheated on their income tax, and talked about how much they did not like the pastor.

They would say, "I'm born again. I am a Christian. God loves me no matter what I do!"

That is true, but He does not always love or approve of *what* you do. Also, we are not talking about God's attitude; we are talking about *yours*. God may love you, no matter what you do; however, what you say and do proves whether you truly love God or not.

I want to tell you a very important truth:

The level of your love of God is the level of your reception of His Word.

As you commit to God, your love for Him grows and your understanding of His Word also grows. And, vice versa, as you align yourself with His Word, your love of God increases. Words of life will begin to be spoken out of your mouth, not words of death. The abundance of your heart will overflow love.

In the very next verse, John wrote that *the love of and for God* has been perfected in those who keep His message in its entirety. And he added:

> **Whosever says he abides in Him ought — as a personal debt — to walk and conduct himself in the same way in which He walked and conducted Himself.**
>
> **1 John 2:6 AMP**

And John makes the point more than once in those three short letters that he is not giving them any new words. Loving God and loving your neighbor have been commandments from God since the very beginning, he wrote. Yet, John said, this *is* new in a sense, because when you walked in darkness, you not only could not do it, you could not understand it. (1 John 2:7.)

Love Never Fails

When something bad happens to someone who has offended us or someone we do not approve of, and we think it serves them right, we grieve the Holy Spirit. That kind of attitude stops the flow of His power through us. The heart of God breaks over those who are damned by their own hatred. It is not God's will for anyone to go to Hell. (2 Pet. 3:9.)

If someone does something to you, pray for him. When someone speaks ill of you, you should go into intercession immediately. You should not to want them to have heart attacks, car wrecks, lose their jobs, and be judged of God.

There are preachers across the land on television and in pulpits threatening, "Touch not the anointed of God" (1 Chron. 16:22), and that is true. But it is up to God to enforce it, not us. We must not take on the persona that we are some kind of super gods ourselves, and that if you touch us, calamity will fall on you. (The "touch" might be a manure delivery!)

God also said that vengeance is His. (Heb. 10:30.) We should be on our knees weeping over those who are coming against ministries and Christians, even within the Church, because of the potential evil from Satan to which they are opening themselves. We should not be praying or wishing it onto them.

No wonder we are not getting a harvest. We are not walking in love, even if we have a clear understanding of all of the other steps from planting to reaping.

John wrote:

> **By this** (one who does not practice sinning) **it is made clear who take their nature from God and are His children, and who take their nature from the devil and are his children: no one who does not practice righteousness — who does not conform to God's will in purpose, thought and action — is of God; neither is any one who does not love his brother [his fellow believer in Christ].**
>
> **Because this is the message — the announcement — which you have heard from the first, that we should love one another.**
>
> **1 John 3:10,11** AMP

I have heard people say, "I'm just trying to figure out God's will for my life."

His will is for you to obey Him *and* love Him and your neighbor. When you get committed to the love walk, it will release the promises of God. Many Christians cannot believe "there is no more condemnation for sin" (Rom. 8:1), because they do not know how to love.

They feel guilty, because love is not flowing through them. They do not love, so they cannot believe they *are* loved. They do not even love the Word of God.

The best explanation of love, of course, is in the Apostle Paul's first letter to the Corinthians.

> **If I [can] speak in the tongues of men and [even] of angels, but have not love [that reasoning, intentional, spiritual devotion such as is inspired by God's love for and in us], I am only a noisy gong or a clanging cymbal.**
>
> **And if I have prophetic powers — that is, the gift of interpreting the divine will and purpose; and understand all the secret truths and mysteries and possess all knowledge, and if I have (sufficient) faith so that I can remove mountains, but have not love [God's love in me] I am nothing — a useless nobody.**
>
> **Even if I dole out all that I have [to the poor in providing] food, and if I surrender my body to be burned [or in order that I may glory], but have not love [God's love in me], I gain nothing.**
>
> **Love endures long and is patient and kind; love never is envious nor boils over with jealousy; is not boastful or vainglorious, does not display itself haughtily.**
>
> **It is not conceited — arrogant and inflated with pride; it is not rude (unmannerly), and does not act unbecomingly. Love [God's love in us] does not insist on its own rights or its own way, for it is not self-seeking; it is not touchy or fretful or resentful; it takes no account of the evil done to it — pays no attention to a suffered wrong.**

It does not rejoice at injustice and unrighteousness, but rejoices when right and truth prevail.

Love bears up under anything and everything that comes, is ever ready to believe the best of every person, its hopes are fadeless under all circumstances and it endures everything [without weakening].

Love never fails — never fades out or becomes obsolete or comes to an end. As for prophecy [that is, the gift of interpreting the divine will and purpose], it will be fulfilled and pass away; as for tongues, they will be destroyed and cease; as for knowledge, it will pass away [that is, it will lose its value and be superseded by truth].

For our knowledge is fragmentary (incomplete and imperfect), and our prophecy (our teaching) is fragmentary (incomplete and imperfect).

But when the complete and perfect [total] comes, the incomplete and imperfect will vanish away — become antiquated, void and superseded.

When I was a child, I talked like a child, I thought like a child, I reasoned like a child; now that I have become a man, I am done with childish ways and have put them aside.

For now we are looking in a mirror that gives only a dim (blurred) reflection [of reality as in a riddle or enigma], but then [when perfection comes] we shall see in reality and face to face! Now I know in part (imperfectly); but then I shall know and understand fully and clearly, even in the same manner as I have been fully and clearly known and understood [by God].

And so faith, hope, love abide; [faith, conviction and belief respecting man's relation to God and divine things; hope, joyful and confident expectation of eternal salvation; love, true affection for God and man, growing out of God's love for and in us], these three, but the greatest of these is love.

1 Corinthians 13:1-13 AMP

In addition to Jesus, the Apostles Paul and John wrote the most about love. And those two certainly had among the greatest harvests of any of the disciples of Jesus. Paul was not one of the twelve, but he described himself as one born out of due time. (1 Cor. 15:8.)

Those two men also had as many or more opportunities in their lives to get out of the love walk as anyone except Jesus. Paul said he had been beaten five times and beaten with rods twice, stoned once, shipwrecked three times, sick, poor at times, experienced many perils, and finally ended up in prison. (2 Cor. 11:25.) Yet he could write 1 Corinthians 13, the greatest description of love in the Bible.

The Romans attempted to boil John in oil, but early Church legends have it that, like Daniel in the lions' den, he was preserved. Finally, they are supposed to have put his eyes out. We know he was confined as an old man on a barren island, called Patmos. (Rev. 1:9.) There he is said to have been fastened to mining equipment to pull it like a mule, day after day.

Yet he saw the greatest revelation of Jesus ever shown to mankind — the last book in the Bible. Why? Because through all of the trials, tribulations, and hardships, he understood love. He understood how to "bless and curse not" those who did evil to him.

He understood that whatever he sowed, he would also reap.

He understood that you do not pour poison out of your reservoir at other people and expect to bring in a harvest of love.

He understood that you bless those who despitefully use you for the sake of Jesus' name, for "great will be your reward in heaven."

> But love ye your enemies, and do good, and lend,
> hoping for nothing again; and your reward shall be
> great, and ye shall be the children of the Highest: for
> he is kind unto the unthankful and to the evil.
>
> **Luke 6:35**

He understood that it is no credit to you to love those who love you or to do good to those who do good to you. (Luke 6:32,33.) Even those without God can do that. That is normal, human nature, and it is easy.

He understood that his words were like fire and his tongue contained the power of life and death.

He understood his destiny and how to put in the sickle for a harvest: strategy, insight, cultivation, kinetic energy, and love.

And, last of all, both John and Paul understood endurance. When they had done all to stand, they stood until the harvest came.

8

Endurance: Waiting for the Harvest

... And having done all, to stand.

Stand therefore, having your loins girt about with truth, and having on the breastplate of righteousness;

And your feet shod with the preparation of the gospel of peace;

Above all, taking the shield of faith, wherewith ye shall be able to quench all the fiery darts of the wicked.

Ephesians 6:13-16

Every farmer knows that seed in his hand represents life. When he plants that seed, bears up courageously during bad weather, bad economic times, and bad infestations of insects, and *endures to the end*, he will bring in a harvest.

Matthew 24:13 says:

But he that shall endure unto the end, the same shall be saved.

Endure means "to wait patiently or to bear up courageously under hardships or persecution." The Greek word for *saved* in that verse is *soteria*, the totality of salvation. So what Jesus was saying is that those who bear up courageously in the midst of the storms of life will be saved from all of them. The context is the evil days of endtimes.

93

He might have said, "He who maintains faith and walks in love through all of the evil days, he who stays under the Word of God and does not move out from under its protection, will be saved out of all of his troubles."

Not long ago I read an article on the things most Americans want in 1994. They are:

1. More money

2. Health

3. Happiness.

If you are one of those who would list your desires this way, then you need to catch hold of the instruction available in this book. You should get hold of these truths from the Word of God the way a shipwrecked sailor would a plank in the middle of the ocean.

Consider a sailor on life's seas, shipwrecked and with everything else gone — but fifty yards away is a "plank." He will grab hold of that and *endure* through winds, current, and sharks. He will bear up courageously under all conditions and never, never let go of the plank. It will be his salvation.

What is that plank?

Solomon wrote:

> **Take fast hold of instruction; let her not go: keep her; for she is thy life.**
>
> **Proverbs 4:13**

Instruction is knowledge from the Word of God which, Solomon also wrote, will bring length of days, long life, and peace. And he said that length of days, riches, and honor are in the right hand of *wisdom*. You cannot gain wisdom without instruction.

Proverbs 3:18 says that **happy is every one that retaineth her** (wisdom). So you see those three most-wanted things are all found in the seed, the Word of God. Plant it in your life as instruction, and the green shoots of wisdom will spring up, bringing a harvest of prosperity, health, and happiness.

Understanding seed is making sense of the Word of God. The Church has had problems for centuries because too many leaders have not made sense of the Word of God. They have not sought instruction and wisdom, so they have planted few seeds.

If we have followed God's spiritual laws, then we *can* expect a harvest. It is not wrong to look for a harvest!

In the natural, when a farmer plants generously and has an abundant harvest:

Do we picket his farm when he harvests bushels and bushels of corn? Perhaps he got a thousand-fold return or more.

Do people run around talking about him saying, "He's not spiritual. He is carnal. He is always thinking about material things"?

Do we think and say, "He must have done something wrong, or he would not have that much; maybe he stole it"?

Do we walk up to him and say, "What do you think you are doing with two ears of corn for that one seed"?

My wife was talking recently to a friend about how her daughter could get her needs met, and she asked the woman if the daughter was sowing financial seeds.

"Well, no," she said.

How can she then expect to get her needs met in the Lord? She must plant the seed of the Word, then express that seed in the tangible form of money, in order to get a harvest of money in return.

If You Do Not Sow, You Cannot Reap

If you are not sowing, how can you expect to reap?

It will do no good to sit back, look at the soil, and command "Grow! God, make it grow. If You love me, You will make it grow."

God does love you, but if you do not plant, you do not reap. Many times, people do not put the seed in the ground at all, or they keep pulling it up to see if it is growing.

Some say, "If I sow expecting a harvest, I will be greedy, or I will come across that way. I am afraid people will think I have impure motives."

Do you have impure motives? If so, repent; if not, do not worry about what people think. Do what God says to do. Plant the seed, because in it is *life*.

Once you have planted and kept the birds from eating up your seed or the insects from destroying the plants, then set yourself to endure until harvest time.

In the waiting part of this process, we can "sow" into someone else's harvest by helping them endure. Again, we can cultivate our own by encouraging someone else.

All of us need someone to pat us on the back and say, "Just hold on, brother, we're going to do it for Jesus. Just endure until the end, and you will be saved by the harvest of whatever you have sown."

Since the Lord gave me understanding and instruction, I operate according to His wisdom:

- I plant, knowing that if I faint not, I will harvest.

- I keep my "soil" watered with the Word of God, knowing that it is the seed that already is watered with an anointing.

- I have my *sickle* ready and sharpened by having a strategy, operating on insight from the Holy Spirit, cultivating other's gardens, keeping my turbine clean and in working order, turning the power on through walking in love, and then, standing and standing and standing however long it takes to win.

I set myself to bear up courageously against whatever comes against me to steal my seed, because in my seed is life. If I do not protect it, I will "starve" in that area.

- I keep the vision God has given me clear in my mind.

If we looked at "endangered species" in the spiritual realm, seed would be at the top of the list — not the humped-back whale, the horned owl, but the seed. It is endangered in the lives of God's people, because we deal flippantly with it. We do not guard it, protect it, and hold it fast. Too many do not realize that the seed is their life.

We look at natural seeds, and we think, "Man, there is corn, tomatoes, or apples in there. There is potential in these little seeds." Somehow, however, Christians have not looked at the Word of God the same way.

The devil hates seed planters. He hates sowers of the Word, because he knows that whatever a man sows he also is going to reap.

Be not deceived; God is not mocked: for whatsoever a man soweth, that shall he also reap.

> For he that soweth to his flesh shall of the flesh
> reap corruption; but he that soweth to the Spirit shall
> of the Spirit reap life everlasting.
>
> And let us not be weary in well-doing: for in due
> season we shall reap, if we faint not.
>
> Galatians 6:7-9

If we are not being "weary in well-doing," then we are standing. We are enduring until the "due season" comes around.

The average Christian forgets the message (loses the seed) before he gets out of the parking lot after church. You need to take notes, get the tapes and listen over and over, and study the Bible for yourself. You must make yourself knowledgeable concerning seeds.

The Apostle Peter writes three times in 2 Peter 1 of "bringing to mind what those to whom he wrote had been taught."

> Wherefore I will not be negligent to put you
> always in remembrance of these things, though ye
> know them, and be established in the present truth.
>
> Yea, I think it meet, as long as I am in this
> tabernacle (still alive), to stir you up by putting you
> in remembrance.
>
> Moreover I will endeavour that ye may be able
> after my decease to have these things always in
> remembrance.
>
> 2 Peter 1:12,13,15

Put Yourself in Remembrance

Something I have found helpful is to make a cassette tape talking to myself that I can play back when I need to be encouraged and strengthened.

Say, "Good morning, (your name), this is (your name). I want you to know there is a seed in you and a vision from God." Then go on and exhort yourself, preach to yourself.

Write it down and stick it on the refrigerator, stick a card in the edge of the mirror, "I am a seed planter." Write out the verses that are the seed you are planting. Command your thoughts to think only on good things. (Phil. 4:8.)

When you do not feel like enduring, read those cards or play the tape to yourself.

"I am feeling 'down' today" — push play.

"I do not feel like standing" — push play.

"I do not want to hold onto this stuff" — push play.

Standing involves *paying* close attention to what you have heard, lest you drift away from it. What happens when you run across that little word *pay*? You know that it means whatever it is attached to is going to cost you something. Anything to which we pay attention involves a cost.

If I am going to pay more attention to God's Word, it is going to cost me something. That means I have to pay a price, give up something else.

If you do not pay up front, it will cost you double later. Pay closer attention to your vision, to the seed.

Hebrews 10:23 says to "hold fast your confession of faith without wavering." *Hold fast* means "to endure."

The sailor on that plank in the middle of the ocean had to hold onto the plank, for the plank was his lifeline. He held on until the harvest — his rescue — came. He did not let go of that plank until the sure thing came. He did not let go until he knew that he was not hallucinating, seeing a mirage, or making a compromise instead of reaching shore.

Do not let go of your seed for a compromised version of the Gospel. Hold fast to it.

The author of Hebrews wrote:

> **For ye have need of patience** (endurance)**, that, after ye have done the will of God, ye might receive the promise.**
>
> **For yet a little while, and he that shall come will come, and will not tarry.**
>
> **Now the just shall live by faith: but if any man draw back, my soul shall have no pleasure in him.**
> **Hebrews 10:36-38**

How is the Church going to minister to sick people, if we are all sick?

How are we ever going to help those in a divorced situation, if all of our marriages are falling apart?

How are we ever going to help the lost children in the world, if our own children are full of rebellion?

How are we going to offer wisdom, if we cannot think spiritually and our minds are so warped that we do not even know who we are half the time?

How are we going to help the world?

We must learn how to sow seeds and reap harvests in our own lives, before we can be examples — or a light — to the world. If we do not believe the Word of God, how can we expect unbelievers to accept it?

When we truly begin to love God by doing His commandments, the world around us will change. We must be *doers* and not just *hearers*. Christians today have become mostly a Church of "hearers."

> **For not the hearers of the law are just before God, but the *doers* of the law shall be justified.**
> **Romans 2:13**

> But be ye doers of the word, and not hearers only, deceiving your own selves.
>
> For if any be a hearer of the word, and not a doer, he is like unto a man beholding his natural face in a glass:
>
> For he beholdeth himself, and goeth his way, and straightway forgetteth what manner of man he was.
>
> But whoso looketh into the perfect law of liberty, and continueth therein, he being not a forgetful hearer, but a doer of the work, this man shall be blessed in his deed.
>
> **James 1:22-25**

Five "Seeds" To Help You Stand

Did you know that you could sow for endurance?

Here are five "seeds" among thousands that — if you remind yourself of them over and over until they become part of you, deeply buried in the soil of your heart — will help you endure until your harvest comes in.

The first is found in Philippians 2:9-11:

> Wherefore God also hath highly exalted him, and given him a name which is above every name:
>
> That at the name of Jesus every knee should bow, of things in heaven, and things in earth, and things under the earth;
>
> And that every tongue should confess that Jesus Christ is Lord, to the glory of God the Father.

Your confession over this seed could be something like:

"I confess and declare today that Jesus Christ is the Lord of my life, completely. In every situation, time, and place, He is Lord. He is in control."

Seed number two is embedded in 1 Peter 5:6,7:

Humble yourselves therefore under the mighty hand of God, that he may exalt you in due time:

Casting all your care upon him; for he careth for you.

Your confession based on these verses would be something like this:

"I have humbled myself and cast the care of everything in my life on Jesus, because He loves me, and I love Him. I will endure until the harvest and not take thought or worry for anything." (Matt. 6:34.)

The third seed is found in Psalm 23:1:

The Lord is my shepherd; I shall not want.

"I have no lack today in my life.

"I have no wants that God cannot meet.

"I can do all things through Christ Who strengthens me. (Phil. 4:13.)

"Jesus is the Shepherd who carries all of the worry for me. I must just follow where He leads."

The fourth seed is in two parts — Isaiah 53:3-5 and 1 Peter 2:24:

He is despised and rejected of men; a man of sorrows, and acquainted with grief: and we hid as it were our faces from him; he was despised, and we esteemed him not.

Surely he hath borne our griefs, and carried our sorrows: yet we did esteem him stricken, smitten of God, and afflicted.

But he was wounded for our transgressions, he was bruised for our iniquities: the chastisement of our

peace was upon him; and with his stripes we *are* healed.

Who his own self bare our sins in his own body on the tree, that we, being dead to sins, should live unto righteousness: by whose stripes ye *were* healed.

These verses are seed not only for healing but for maintaining health. Sometimes this is called "walking in divine health." Make up your own confession along the following lines, memorize it and repeat it to yourself throughout the day. Put it on tape to play it back, and write it on cards to put in places where your eyes will have to see it.

"I have health in my body, because Jesus took all of the sicknesses and diseases for my sake almost two thousand years ago when He was beaten.

"I have health in my spirit, because He took my sins on the cross at Calvary.

"I have a healthy mind and emotions, because I am dead to sin and live through His righteousness, because He took the filthy rags of self-righteousness (Isa. 64:6) for His pure robe of righteousness.

"I have planted these seeds from the Bible, and I will reap healing and health if I faint not."

Seed number five is 1 Corinthians 1:30,31:

But of him are ye in Christ Jesus, who of God is made unto us wisdom, and righteousness, and sanctification, and redemption:

That, according as it is written, He that glorieth, let him glory in the Lord.

Based on that seed planted in the good soil of your heart, confess this as your harvest:

"Father God, Your Word is life to me. Jesus, You are my sanctification. You set me apart from all evil. You are my wisdom come down from Heaven, Holy Spirit.

"Long life is in You, riches and honor, and peace and happiness dwell within Your gates. You are my redemption, for You have brought me out of the kingdom of darkness into God's marvelous light.

"I am now a citizen of Heaven, and I glory in the Lord, not in my own efforts.

"Thank You, Lord, for the great exchange that took place when I was born again. I took off my coat of sin, failure, impossibilities, inadequacy, pain, and hurt, and You put on me Your robe of righteousness.

"I am a brand-new person in Christ. It is no longer I who lives, but Christ Who lives within me.

"Now, I am ready to face the world. I am ready to deal with the things of this life. I am ready to endure until the harvest. I am sharpening and repairing my sickle.

"With victory in my voice and determination in my heart, I purpose not to bow my knee to the voice of death or to the defeat of the enemy, but only to life. For I am a seed planter and a harvester with a sickle in my hand."

Are you willing to pay the price for excellence?

Are you willing to pay the attention required to really make a mark that cannot be erased?

Are you willing to pay the price to have your life changed?

You may have a vision, but it is in seed form, and seeds do not pay bills. Seed does not go to market. But when the harvest comes, it goes to market, and it pays your bills. You will reap according to what you have sown in the beginning.

> **And God said, Let the earth bring forth grass, the herb yielding seed, and the fruit tree yielding fruit after his kind, whose seed is in itself, upon the earth: and it was so.**
>
> **Genesis 1:11**

From the beginning, the process of reproduction of everything started from a seed which has in it the life of the next generation. God's principles are true in every realm, physical, mental, emotional, and spiritual. We saw in Galatians 6:8 that sowing to the flesh (sin) reaps corruption (death or destruction).

The choice is entirely up to you, whether to give up on your harvest or to stand until the seed bears fruit. I want you to know, however, that victory in the harvest destroys the enemy. *The devil tries to destroy the seed, before the fruit of it destroys him.*

In the next chapter, we are going to look at "tares" and other ways the enemy tries to destroy your harvest.

9

Endurance Destroys the Enemy

> . . . The kingdom of heaven is likened unto a man
> which sowed good seed in his field:
>
> But while men slept, his enemy came and sowed
> tares among the wheat, and went his way.
>
> So the servants of the householder came and said
> unto him, Sir, didst not thou sow good seed in thy
> field? from whence then hath it tares?
>
> He said unto them, An enemy hath done this. . . .
> Matthew 13:24,25,27,28

If the Word of God is good seed, what are "tares"? They also are seed. So we see from Matthew 13:24-30 that just as there is godly seed sown in good soil, there can be ungodly seed also sown. And the tares and weeds look just like the wheat.

And Jesus said, "Don't tear them up, or pull them up, in case you get some of the wheat by accident, or disrupt its growing. Let them grow alongside one another until the harvest. We will separate the wheat and the tares later."

The sowing of tares is what the devil does to try and choke out the good seed. If God's words are seed, so are the devil's. If good seed has a potential for growth, so does bad seed.

107

But where God's seed has a potential for life, the devil's potential is for death. However, both seeds grow and produce a harvest.

If I am to hold fast to the Word of God like a shipwrecked sailor in the middle of the ocean, then I need to loose or let go of the seed of the devil trying to germinate in my life. If I hold onto it, it will take root in me and produce death of some kind.

In the parable Jesus told in Matthew 13, He is talking about the Church and instructing His servants not to try to pull up the weeds (ungodly people who are masquerading as Christians, "spots and blemishes" in the Body — 2 Pet. 2:13) until the final harvest, when He will separate the sheep from the goats. (Matt. 25:32,33.)

However, in our own lives, we must pull up the weeds in order that they will not choke out the harvest. (Matt. 13:7.)

Satan wants to destroy your vision in its embryonic state, because it means his death warrant in your life if it matures.

The late Walt Disney's dream only became a source of financial power when it became mature. While it was only in his mind and on paper, it was only a dream. But once it began to be successful, the stock market picked up on it, and there emerged power in the dream.

While it was still only on paper, you might have talked him out of it. Perhaps you could have stolen his vision. You could have planted seed to choke it out through discouragement, worry, and cares. At that point, it could have been destroyed.

The devil knows this principle better than we do. Once we get the fruit from our vision, he cannot stop us. He needs to take you out before you get into full-time ministry, and before you move into the fullness of the harvest of your seed.

Walk by Faith and Not by Sight

All you and I have is *seed*. In fact, that is all God had! His words spoken forth resulted in a harvest of the universe, the heavenlies, the earth and all of its plants and creatures, and mankind.

You may say, "I only have one promise. I only have one Word."

That is all you need; that is all God had: **In the beginning was the Word** (John 1:1).

If you sow the Word of God and do the will of God in spite of what you see, what you hear, what you feel, and what you taste, then you will reap the promise of what God declared to be. That's what it means by "walking by faith and not by sight." (2 Cor. 5:7.)

When I got hold of the fact that the enemy must kill or destroy the seed during the germination time, I said, "Lord! That old rascal has been faking me out. I didn't realize what he was doing. Why, he's running scared because I have made declarations. I have sown seed in my future that he knows will produce, because it has potential in it."

So the enemy works harder, and it gets darker. He works, and your life gets harder. You can know you are on the right track when the devil is doing everything he can to choke that thing out of you. Special demonic warriors armed with fiery darts come in to sow seeds of death to choke out the seed of life in you.

Psalm 1:3 speaks of what the man is like who meditates day and night upon the seed:

> **And he shall be like a tree planted by the rivers of water, that bringeth forth his fruit in his season; his leaf also shall not wither; and whatsoever he doeth shall prosper.**

The devil does not want our seed to become leafy, mature, and bear fruit. The promise fulfilled brings healing to the people. Revelation 22:1 talks about a river of life with a tree beside it bearing twelve kinds of fruit and the leaves are for the healing of the nations. That is God's vision fulfilled, come to harvest.

In miniature, in each of our lives, the vision from God will bring healing to your life and those around you. Satan knows he must abort that vision somewhere along the line, because if you mature and get leaves and fruit, you will "heal the nations."

He is scared to death. He knows that when you and I are persistent, do not quit, maintain our stand, and guard the seed, his days are numbered.

A seed does not have any leaves nor any fruit. When you eat an apple, you spit out the seeds. And you are spitting out hundreds of apples, because the life of that apple is in the seed.

Would you like to know how to be persecuted? Sow seed, and stand for the harvest.

Would you like to know how not to be persecuted? Sit down, do not sow seed, do nothing for the Lord, and bear no fruit. Then you will be no threat to the devil.

When you are determined to work adamantly at your vision, people will persecute you. But if you are lazy about it, you will not be persecuted. You will be welcomed and patted on the back, because you are just like those around you in the world.

I know three ways to become persecuted:

• Be determined. People hate other people who are determined not to fail.

• Be "fired up" for God. That makes people uncomfortable.

• Be overtly ambitious in your goals. Most people are more comfortable with mediocrity than with excellence.

Have a desire, but no fire; have a good talk, but not a good walk, and you will not be a threat to the enemy.

If you determine to stand against his onslaughts, he will send his "special forces" that are very rude and demanding. They will be hot in pursuit to destroy that seed in you.

Why are we told to use the shield of faith? (Eph. 6:16.) We need the shield of faith because the words or acts of those special forces will be aimed at your conscious mind to destroy the potential of the seed, to discourage you from planting it.

You have to have a shield of faith to stop the fiery darts of Satan's attacks.

When an exiled Jew named Nehemiah was led by God to help rebuild Jerusalem after Judah's seventy-year sojourn in Babylon was over, the Word of God was a seed that he planted, protected, and guarded to harvest. That Word had been given to the prophets.

> **Know therefore and understand, that from the going forth of the commandment to restore and to build Jerusalem unto the Messiah the Prince shall be seven weeks, and threescore and two weeks: the street shall be built again,** *and the wall,* **even in troublous times.**
>
> **Daniel 9:25**

God Chooses the Vessel and the Seed

Nehemiah had a seed planted in his heart by God:

> **That Hanani, one of my brethren, came, he and certain men of Judah; and I asked them concerning the Jews that had escaped, which were left of the captivity, and concerning Jerusalem.**
>
> **And they said unto me, The remnant that are left of the captivity there in the province are in great affliction and reproach: the wall of Jerusalem also is broken down, and the gates thereof are burned with fire.**
>
> **And it came to pass, when I heard these words, that I sat down and wept, and mourned certain days, and fasted, and prayed before the God of heaven.**
>
> **Nehemiah 1:2-4**

Nehemiah got a vision from God. He had a destiny, determined by God for him before the foundation of the world. That destiny was to be the one who carried out the rebuilding of the wall, thus fulfilling God's promise to those Jews who returned from exile in Babylon.

Why did God pick Nehemiah? We cannot always see why God chooses this one or that one to do certain things. But there are some things we do know:

• Only God knows what seed has been planted in each Christian at conversion.

• Only God knows the place and position each of us will be in to carry out part of His plan.

• Only God knew before He made the world and everything in it that Nehemiah would become the "cup-bearer" of the King of Persia, who conquered Babylon. (Neh. 2:1.)

• Only God knew that Nehemiah would have the official standing, as one who stood before the king daily and had his favor, to get supplies and fend off other enemy officials who wanted to keep Judah weak. (Neh. 2:5-9.)

• Only God knew that Nehemiah would have the spiritual strength and determination to keep everyone else working together in unity and standing until the harvest, which was the completion of the rebuilding of the wall.

God knows everything from beginning to end ahead of time, and He chooses who is to plant apples and who is to plant potatoes. Paul explained this another way when he wrote about the Body of Christ in terms of the human body: Some are toes, some are fingers, and so forth. (1 Cor. 12:12-27; Eph. 4:15,16.)

You do not choose what kind of turbine (vessel) you are. You can only choose whether to obey God and operate in being the kind He has made you.

> **But now hath God set the members every one of them in the body, as it *hath pleased him*.**
> **1 Corinthians 12:18**

Nehemiah wept when the "seed" hit him. He wept because the Word had not taken root in those exiles who had returned, and he chose to accept the seed for himself. (Neh. 1:4-11.)

The seed took root in Nehemiah's heart, and when he went out to bring forth fruit, he made the non-Jews around Jerusalem angry. This was especially true of a Horonite named Sanballat, who became the devil's "front man" to stop the work.

Nehemiah's Harvest Overcame the Enemy

> **But it came to pass, that when Sanballat heard that we builded the wall, he was wroth, and took great indignation, and mocked the Jews.**

> **And he spake before his brethren and the army
> of Samaria, and said, What do these feeble Jews? will
> they fortify themselves? will they sacrifice? will they
> make an end in a day? will they revive the stones out
> of the heaps of the rubbish which are burned?**
>
> **Now Tobiah the Ammonite was by him, and he
> said, Even that which they build, if a fox go up, he
> shall even break down their stone wall.**
>
> **Nehemiah 4:1-3**

In the original Hebrew, it says that "Sanballat
became jealous." But while he and his friends were
making fun and being highly critical, the returned Jews
kept right on building stone by stone. Sanballat blazed
with jealousy and mocked the Jews. He was provoked
to action to destroy the wall.

He and a number of others conspired to fight the
wall builders and hinder it. (Neh. 4:7,8.) The enemy was
filled with jealousy, provoked to action, and mocked
the Jews. This is a picture of what the devil does when
we begin to fulfill our visions.

They walked around acting like Nehemiah,
pretending to make the same declaration he did, but
in a mocking way; in other words, imitating Nehemiah
to scorn.

Nehemiah 4:2 relates that Sanballat said to his
brothers and the wealthy men of Samaria, "What do
these feeble Jews think they are doing?"

Feeble means "languid, listless, lacking animation,
indisposed toward physical exertion." In other words,
he was calling them "lazy jerks."

He was saying, "These people lack drive. They will
never do what they say they are going to do. They talk
big, but do little. They are not ambitious. They basically

are uneducated people who know nothing about building walls.

"They do not even have building materials. All they have is ash and rubbish. (Neh. 4:10.) How are they going to build strong, sturdy walls?"

God only had dust when He created Adam and Eve. You do not need tangible resources stored up in a bank account to build a church.

All you need is faith to obey what God has told you to do.

All you need is a reformed life based on the power of the Holy Spirit and washed by the blood of Jesus.

All you need is a redeemed portion of life, and God can take the rubbish and ashes, and breathe life into it.

Part of the way through the building of the wall, the people began to get discouraged. That was the point at which they needed to begin to stand. Here was where they needed *endurance* to destroy the enemy.

In verse 10, it says that the strength of the burden bearers was failing, there was too much rubbish to move, and the people were confessing that they were unable to build the wall. The workers were failing. They had lost their faith and gotten tired, and were ready to give up. A discouraged man is useless, and the devil knows it.

You may feel like that about your life. Your failures, the broken parts of your life, the smashed rubbish of past visions and dreams that lie around you are under your feet. You have two choices: Sit down, rub ashes on your head, and cry "Woe is me," or get up, take the ash which is rich in nitrogen, mix it with your seed, and turn the care over to God, Who brings the increase.

God Builds With the Debris of Our Lives

Remember, in an earlier chapter, we saw that the *best* thing to make a garden grow was manure. You need to understand that when we do not have anything, when we are unable to rebuild part of our life, God says, "Just get out of the way. I'll take the ash out of your experience, breathe life into it, and create something out of nothing."

The last thing God wants is your resources *or* mine. He just wants our failures, our broken pieces, the fragments of our lives. He is going to crush them down real fine. Then when the devil thinks he is destroying you, God is really creating dust. Out of it will come a living, strong, and powerful harvest.

Nehemiah got hold of the situation. He encouraged the people. (Neh. 4:14.) He encouraged them by reminding them that they served a "great and terrible" God Who fought for them.

So what if you are tired?

So what if you are a failure on your own?

So what if all you have to build with is rubbish?

It is God's strength and might that will bring the increase anyway, not yours.

The enemies heard that God had brought their counsel to nought and that everyone turned to working again on the walls, holding spears in one hand and building tools in the other. (Neh. 4:16-18.) The people began to see the end result. They got a vision of the harvest.

You will get a mind, or a will, to work as soon as you realize that God is for you, not against you, and when you can see the harvest.

Nehemiah guarded the project against acts of aggression that would have "choked out the seed in its embryonic state." And when the enemies heard that the wall was built, they tried to lure Nehemiah out of the city to kill him, but he did not fall for that.

The next attack was to pronounce a prophecy against him that he would be killed. But Nehemiah perceived that God had not sent this "prophet" to speak against him but that he was a "hired gun" sent to make him afraid by an evil report. (Neh. 6:10-14.)

You have to watch out for those, sometimes even family members and friends, who speak discouragement, doubt, and fear into your harvest. Without realizing it, many become "hired guns" for the enemy to try and abort your harvest. Forgive them, and pay no attention to their words when you know that God has given you the vision and is fighting your battles.

Again, there is that word *pay*. If you do "pay attention" to their words, it will cost you, perhaps even the entire harvest.

The wall was finished, and the enemy was "much cast down in their own eyes" and saw that the work was done by God. (Neh. 6:15,16.)

Nehemiah's work had not been in vain.

If we will endure until the end, our work will not have been in vain. Paul wrote:

> **Therefore, my beloved brethren, be ye stedfast, unmoveable, always abounding in the work of the Lord, forasmuch as ye know that your labour is not in vain in the Lord.**
>
> **1 Corinthians 15:58**

Summary

Your toil, your enduring, your bearing up under persecution, ridicule, and suspicion, your protecting the seed from the enemy will not have been in vain if you do not give up before the harvest.

But until you are convinced that God is able to bring the Word you received to maturity, you can be defeated. Paul also suffered these things, as we saw earlier, yet he said he was not ashamed. (2 Tim. 1:12.) He knew in Whom he believed, and Paul was convinced that God was able to guard that which was entrusted to Him until the dream was fulfilled.

I am convinced that the seed God has entrusted to me will be brought to maturity. Second Timothy 1:13 says to "retain the standard of sound words."

You are not just marking time to the rapture or to the time when you go to be with the Lord in Heaven.

You are not just "enduring" the trials and tribulations because that is the normal state of a Christian — to be downtrodden, poor, and defeated.

You are here for a purpose. You were chosen by God as His child to carry out His will and His plans. You are to "endure" for a purpose, and that is victory, not defeat.

Second Peter 1:10,11 says:

> **Wherefore the rather, brethren, give diligence to make your calling and election sure: for if ye do these things, ye shall never fall:**
>
> **For so an entrance shall be ministered unto you abundantly into the everlasting kingdom of our Lord and Savior Jesus Christ.**

In the first part of that chapter, Peter wrote that the divine power of Jesus had given us all things *that* pertain to life and godliness, and he listed eight things that are in us through Christ Jesus. They are:

- Diligence (working consistently)
- Faith (belief in God and His Word)
- Virtue (morality)
- Knowledge (instruction)
- Temperance (moderation)
- Patience (endurance)
- Godliness (righteousness)
- Brotherly kindness and charity (love)

He said that if these things abound in us, they will make us *neither barren nor unfruitful.*

The final promise to those who plant seed in obedience to the seed planted in them and who stand until the harvest is found in Revelation 21:7 AMP:

> **He who is victorious shall inherit all these things,**
> **and I will be God to him and he shall be My son.**

The *King James Version* translates that verse this way:

> **He that *overcometh* shall inherit all things; and**
> **I will be his God, and he shall be my son.**

Victorious means enduring until the end. It means "overcoming" the world, flesh, and the devil to fulfill your vision from God. *These things* that we will inherit include: the holy city, no more death, sorrow, pain, or tears, and eternal life ("drinking of the water of life freely") with the Godhead.

A "seed" that sums up where a Christian stands is found in Romans 8, and this one passage spoken as a confession until it becomes *truth* to you will illuminate your understanding of seed as perhaps nothing else will.

> For the law of the Spirit of life in Christ Jesus hath made me free from the law of sin and death.
>
> For they that are after the flesh do mind the things of the flesh; but that they are after the Spirit the things of the Spirit.
>
> For to be carnally minded is *death*; but to be spiritually minded is *life and peace*.
>
> Because the carnal mind is enmity against God: for it is not subject to the law of God, neither indeed can be.
>
> So then they that are in the flesh cannot please God.
>
> But ye are not in the flesh, but in the Spirit, if so be that the Spirit of God dwell in you. . . .
>
> For if ye live after the flesh, ye shall die: but if ye through the Spirit do mortify the deeds of the body (take up your cross daily and die to self), ye shall live.
>
> For as many as are led by the Spirit of God, they are the sons of God.
>
> **Romans 8:2,5-9,13,14**

Add this to the five seeds I gave you in the previous chapter, and it will bring life to your heart:

"I have been made free from the law of sin and death. I live after the Spirit and pay attention to the things of the Spirit.

"I am not carnally minded (and make wrong choices). I cast down those imaginations and high thoughts that elevate themselves against the Word of God (2 Cor. 10:5), because they are enemies to God.

"I pull up and cast out those fiery darts of doubt, fear, and unbelief that come from the enemy to destroy my crop, because God did not give me a spirit of bondage to fear but He gave me the Spirit of adoption. (Rom. 8:15)

"I have Christ in me, which means my body is dead to sin — and I make choices each day to walk in the truth of this.

"I am a child of God and a joint-heir with Christ, and I suffer with Him by denying self and obeying His will with cheerfulness and willingness. (Rom. 8:17.)

I pray that this book will change your life. I pray for each reader, that you will not quit, but persevere; not escape, but endure. The good work God has begun in you, He will complete, if you will allow Him.

I pray with you that you will be able to fulfill the vision God has given you, and that you will plant abundantly and reap abundantly. Remember, Jesus said, "I have come that you might have life, and have it more abundantly."